Writing from Within 1

Second Edition

Curtis Kelly & Arlen Gargagliano

CAMBRIDGE UNIVERSITY PRESS
Cambridge, New York, Melbourne, Madrid, Cape Town,
Singapore, São Paulo, Dehli, Mexico City

Cambridge University Press
32 Avenue of the Americas, New York, NY 10013-2473, USA

www.cambridge.org
Information on this title: www.cambridge.org/9780521188272

First published 2011
2nd printing 2012

Printed in Hong Kong, China, by Golden Cup Printing Company Limited

A catalog record for this publication is available from the British Library.

Library of Congress Cataloging-in-Publication Data
Kelly, Curtis.
Writing from within. 1 / Curtis Kelly & Arlen Gargagliano. — 2nd ed.
p. cm.
ISBN 978-0-521-18827-2 (alk. paper)
1. English language—Textbooks for foreign speakers. 2. English
language—Rhetoric. 3. English language—Paragraphs. I. Gargagliano,
Arlen. II. Title.
PE1128.K418624 2011
808'.042—dc22
2011014846

ISBN 978-0-521-18827-2 Student's Book
ISBN 978-0-521-18831-9 Teacher's Manual

Book design and photo research: TSI Graphics
Layout services: Page Designs International, Inc.

Illustration credits: pages 2, 17, 20–21, 37, 41–46, 50–51, 71, 91–101, 109 Li Dan; pages 11, 13, 30–31, 40, 61–65, 75, 111
Albert Tan; pages 23, 80–85, 106, 120 TSI Graphics.

Photo credits: 4 ©iStockphoto.com/Jacom Stephens; 6 DAJ/Getty Images; 8 ©iStockphoto.com/Justin Horrocks; 9 ©lightpoet*;
10 ©Lane V. Erickson*; 12 Panoramic Images/Getty Images; 15 (t to b) ©erashov*, ©Kristin Smith*, ©iStockphoto.com/williv
©cristi180884*; 16 Richard I'Anson/Lonely Planet Images; 18 ©iStockphoto.com/36clicks; 19 Robert Harding Picture Library/
SuperStock; 22 Masterfile Royalty Free; 24 ©Dmitriy Shironosov*; 25 ©Kenneth Mann*; 26 Masterfile Royalty Free; 29 (l to r)
©Supri Suharjoto*, ©DenisNata*, ©iStockphoto.com/Hakan Caglav, ©Stephen Coburn*; 32 Ryan McVay/Getty Royalty Free;
34 (t to b) ©bikeriderlondon*, Jon Feingersh/Getty Images, ©Andrew F. Kazmierski*; 35 ©Cristophe Testi*; 36 H. Armstrong
Roberts/Getty Images; 38 ©Mikhail*; 39 ©Yuri Arcurs*; 45 (l to r, t to b) ©Iakiv Pekarskyi*, ©Alex Staroseltsev*, ©Volosina*,
©Atlaspix*, ©3DSguru*; 52 Masterfile Royalty Free; 54 (t to b) ©iStockphoto.com/Stan Rohrer, ©Rob Wilson*; ©loriklaszlo*,
©fotohunter*; 56 ©Goodluz*; 59 ©Christopher Edwin Nuzzaco*; 62 ©Uros Jonic*; 67 ©29september*; 69 ©LVV*; 72 Photos
12/Alamy; 74 Pictorial Press Ltd/Alamy; 76 AF archive/Alamy; 79 AF archive/Alamy; 82 Stockbyte/Getty Royalty Free;
86 ©Blend Images*; 89 ©Aspen Photo*; 90 ©joyfuldesigns,*; 96 iStockphoto/Thinkstock; 102 Masterfile Royalty Free; 104 (1–4)
©iStockphoto.com/tderden, ©GoodMood Photo*, ©nastiakru*, ©Andy Dean Photography*; 110 (l to r, t to b) ©Tatiana Popova*,
©vovan*, ©Fotocrisis*, ©Ikphotographers*, ©ntwowe*, ©SunnyS*, ©taesmileland*, ©Lipik*, ©Ragnarock*; 112 Hideki Yoshihara/
Photolibrary; 115 Jan Greune/Getty Images; 116 ©Samot,*; 119 ©iStockphoto.com/Linda Kloosterhof.
*2011 Used under license from Shutterstock.com

Contents

Plan of the book

Unit	Writing Assignment
1 Who am I?	An e-mail introducing yourself
2 An important place	One paragraph about an important place and what happened there
3 An ideal partner	One paragraph about your ideal partner
4 My favorite photo	One paragraph about your favorite photo
5 My seal	One paragraph about your seal
6 Party time	One party announcement and one paragraph about a class party
7 Thank-you note	A one-paragraph thank-you note
8 Movie review	A two-paragraph movie review
9 Friendship	Two paragraphs about a friend
10 Superhero powers	Two paragraphs about a superhero power
11 Advertisements	A two-paragraph advertisement
12 Lessons learned	Two paragraphs about an action you regret

Organizational focus	Editing focus	Just for fun assignment
Organizing an e-mail about yourself Adding more information	Connecting sentences	Writing addresses and signatures
Setting the scene Ending a personal story	Using prepositions	Making a guidebook
Listing points Adding reasons	Combining sentences	Playing a matchmaking game
Giving background information Writing a concluding sentence	Mixing past and present tense	Making a photo time line
Organizing information by location Topic sentences	Commas with *because*	Making a group flag
Plans and instructions	*So that* and *to*	Designing a poster for a party
Giving reasons Time markers	*Before, while,* and *after*	Writing a thank-you card
Movie summary Movie opinion	Pronouns	Producing a movie
Supporting sentences	Combining sentences with *so*	Writing an article
Adding examples to a wish	Writing about wishes	Creating a comic book story
Attention getters Testimonials	Using persuasive language	Having a class market
Writing an explanation Conclusions	Word choice	Making a card

To the teacher

For a student who has never written more than a single sentence at a time, drafting a whole paragraph, even a short one, is a daunting challenge. Yet by writing even short texts, a whole new avenue for communication opens up. There are things students will write that they would never say, and writing offers them the potential to go deeply into their inner worlds. We, as authors, believe that all language learners, even low-level learners, possess a need to express themselves and share what is meaningful to them.

This book was written for such learners, especially those we call "3Ls": those low in ability, low in confidence, and low in motivation. Our goal was to create activities that not only allow them to succeed at writing English, but also allow them to express personal, meaningful, and sometimes fanciful facets of their lives. We have tried to create activities that *pull* our learners into writing rather than *push* them.

Writing from Within 1 covers a spectrum of educational objectives. Students are taught how to write sentences, generate and organize content, structure and sequence this content into paragraphs, review and edit what they have written, and finally, how to respond to what others have written. We see writing as a balanced combination of language, expository, and self-revelation skills.

As in *Writing from Within 2*, the focus of each unit is a writing assignment. Some assignments are introspective: For example, learners are asked to reflect on something they are thankful for. Others are more conventional but task-based: Learners are asked to write movie reviews and advertisements. In this way, humanistic writing assignments are balanced with task-based writing assignments to provide a broad range of writing experiences. In addition, each unit ends with an optional expansion activity that gives learners the opportunity to apply their new skills to a different task.

The main task of each unit is the writing assignment. The first six parts of each unit are prewriting activities that have learners generate and organize information, learn basic language structures, and improve their expository skills, such as how to write topic and supporting sentences. Then comes the writing assignment. Following the writing assignment are an editing lesson that helps learners enrich their writing by making stylistic choices, and a feedback lesson, that gives learners the opportunity to respond to their classmates' writing. Each unit takes 3–5 hours of class time to complete, and although the syllabus is developmental, it is not necessary to do each unit in order.

The chart on the following page shows the unit structure.

Prewriting	**Part 1** Brainstorming	*The topic is introduced and writing ideas are generated.*
	Part 2 Analyzing a paragraph	*Students analyze model sentences in the context of a paragraph.*
	Parts 3–5 Learning about organization, Working on content	*Students learn organizational skills and generate content for their paragraphs.*
	Part 6 Analyzing a model	*Students analyze model paragraphs like the ones they will create.*

Writing	**Part 7** Write!	*Students receive instructions for writing their paragraphs.*

Postwriting	**Part 8** Editing	*Students take a closer look at language and structures and edit their writing.*
	Part 9 Giving feedback	*Students exchange paragraphs with other students for review and feedback.*
	Just for Fun	*Students do an optional writing activity that helps them transfer their newly gained skills to a communicative writing task.*

Writing is a skill. We tell our students that learning to write is like learning to play a musical instrument; the more they practice, the better they will be. *Writing from Within 1* is designed to demonstrate to learners that they have the knowledge and ability within to develop this skill. We hope they will enjoy this text, and we look forward to hearing your comments.

Curtis Kelly   Arlen Gargagliano

Acknowledgments

Writing is a process. In this case, *Writing from Within 1* was a process that spanned years and continents. The authors wish to thank the numerous people who helped in the development of this new edition. Particular thanks are owed to the following:

Reviewers and advisors who helped us shape the second edition: Bill Farquharson, King Saud University PY Program, Saudi Arabia; Cara Izumi, University of Washington, ELP, Washington; Heidi Perez, Lawrence Public Schools (K–12), Lawrence Adult Learning Center, Massachusetts; Junil Oh, Pukyong National University, South Korea; Kerry Vrabel, Maricopa Community College, Arizona; Laurie Hartwick, Lawrence High School, Massachusetts; Margarita Mitevska, San Jose City College, California; Todd Squires, Kinki University, Japan; Jack Brajcich, Fukuoka Jogakuin University Junior College; Muriel Fujii, Honolulu Community College, Hawaii; Hiroko Nishikage, Taisho University, Japan; Noriko Hirao, Diego Rael, Paul Raine, and Joseph Robson, OTC, Japan; Shunji Aoki, Kanagawa Institute of Technology, Japan; Michael Stout, Toyo Gakuen University, Japan; Stephen Slater, Centre for English Language in the University of South Australia; Meg Norris, Atlanta, Georgia; and Greg Goodmacher, Keiwa College, Japan.

Cambridge University Press staff and advisors: Caitlin Mara, Bernard Seal, Karen Brock, Debbie Goldblatt, Alan Kaplan, Tami Savir, Sue Andre Costello, Wendy Asplin, Satoko Shimoyama, Harry Ahn, Ivan Sorrentino, Josep Mas, and Heather Ferreyra.

Finally, we would like to thank our families, whose love and patience we continue to depend on.

Who am I?

1 Brainstorming

WHAT IS BRAINSTORMING?

When you brainstorm, you write down as many ideas as you can think of. You can write words, phrases, or sentences.

Words: *tall, manager*

Phrases: *live in Rome, have an older sister*

Sentences: *I'm 32 years old. I have a sports car.*

1 Hakim brainstormed on the question "Who am I?" Read what he wrote.

2 Now brainstorm on the question "Who am I?" Draw a circle on a piece of paper and write your name in the middle. Then write as many words, phrases, and sentences as you can about yourself.

3 Use the information in your brainstorming notes to introduce yourself to a classmate.

> Hi, my name is . . . I am . . .

> **Later in this unit . . .**
>
> You will write an e-mail introducing yourself.
>
> You will also learn how to organize your e-mail, and how to add more information to the topics you write about.

2 Analyzing a paragraph

1 Read the paragraph and follow the instructions below.

(1) My name is Hakim. (2) I am a Saudi man, and I am 32 years old. (3) I live in a small apartment in Rome. (4) I work for an oil company. (5) Someday, I want to have my own business. (6) Tennis is my favorite sport, but I like soccer, too.

a Match the sentences in the paragraph to the topics.

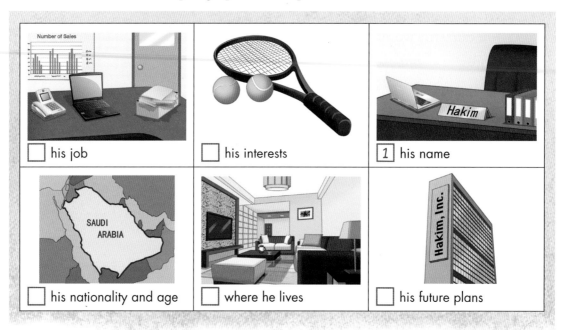

his job

his interests

1 his name

his nationality and age

where he lives

his future plans

b Look at sentence 2 in the paragraph. Write a similar sentence with these words.

Korean man / 20 years old

_____

c Look at sentence 4 in the paragraph. Write a similar sentence with these words.

study English / a university

_____

d Look at sentence 5 in the paragraph. Write a similar sentence with these words.

Someday / have a family

_____

2 Compare answers with a partner.

Talk about it.

Tell your partner about your future plans.

3 Learning about organization

ORGANIZING AN E-MAIL ABOUT YOURSELF

Begin your e-mail with a greeting like those below. Then write a message about who you are, with topics such as your name, age, nationality, gender, etc. End with a closing and your name.

Greeting: *Hi* (name),   *Dear* (name),

Closing: *Thanks,*   *Sincerely,*
           (your name)   (your name)

1 Read the beginning and ending of Tomoko's e-mail introducing herself. Then write similar sentences about yourself below.

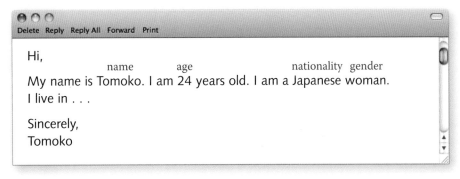

> Delete Reply Reply All Forward Print
>
> Hi,
>   name   age   nationality gender
> My name is Tomoko. I am 24 years old. I am a Japanese woman.
> I live in . . .
>
> Sincerely,
> Tomoko

a Name: *My name is* _____

b Age: _____

c Nationality and gender: _____

2 Now use the sentences above to write the beginning and ending of an e-mail introducing yourself. Use a greeting and a closing from the Word File.

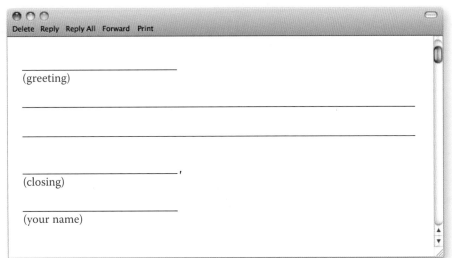

> Delete Reply Reply All Forward Print
>
> _____
> (greeting)
>
> _____
>
> _____
>
> _____ ,
> (closing)
>
> _____
> (your name)

Word File

More Greetings
Hi there!
Hello ☺,

Word File

More Closings
Take care,
Bye,

4 Working on content

1 Read the sentences below. What is the topic of each sentence? Choose a topic from the box. Then write a similar sentence about yourself.

☐ family	☐ future plans	☐ likes and dislikes	☑ school
☐ friends	☐ interests	☐ where you live	☐ job

a I am a junior college student.

Topic: *school*

Your sentence: *I go to a university.*

b I play in a rock band in my free time.

Topic: _____

Your sentence: _____

c I want to be a doctor someday.

Topic: _____

Your sentence: _____

d I work in a coffee shop after school.

Topic: _____

Your sentence: _____

e I live downtown.

Topic: _____

Your sentence: _____

f My best friend is from Singapore.

Topic: _____

Your sentence: _____

g I love classic rock music.

Topic: _____

Your sentence: _____

h I have two sisters and a brother.

Topic: _____

Your sentence: _____

2 Think of one more topic and write a sentence about it.

Topic: _____ Your sentence: _____

5 Learning more about organization

ADDING MORE INFORMATION

Write more than one sentence about each topic in your writing. Add more information to make your writing more interesting.

Sentence	More information
I am a junior college student.	*My major is biology.*
I play in a rock band.	*I play the guitar.*

1 Write a sentence on three topics you would like to put in an e-mail introducing yourself. Then write another sentence with more information for each topic.

a Topic: _____

Sentence: _____

More information: _____

_____

b Topic: _____

Sentence: _____

More information: _____

_____

c Topic: _____

Sentence: _____

More information: _____

_____

2 Work with a partner. Tell your sentences to each other and ask each other questions. Use your discussion to add sentences with more information above.

> I do not have a job. However, I want to get one this summer.

> What kind of job do you want?

6 Analyzing a model

1 You are going to write an e-mail introducing yourself. First, read Tomoko's e-mail and follow the instructions below.

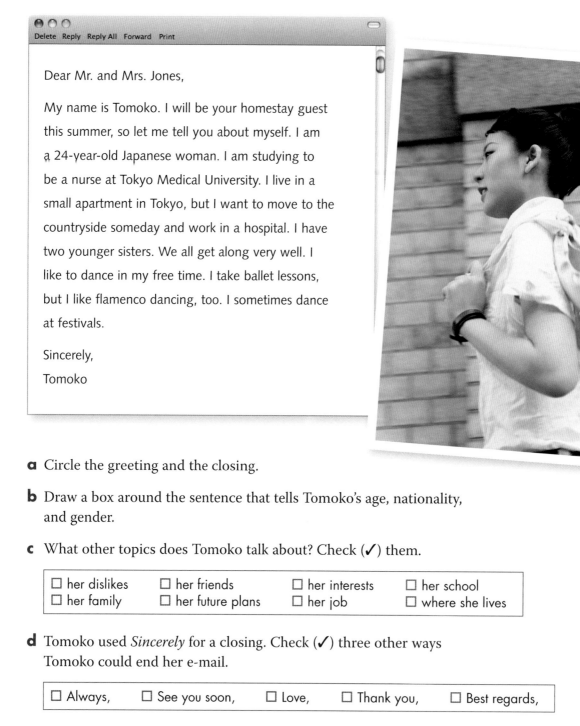

● ○ ○
Delete Reply Reply All Forward Print

Dear Mr. and Mrs. Jones,

My name is Tomoko. I will be your homestay guest this summer, so let me tell you about myself. I am a 24-year-old Japanese woman. I am studying to be a nurse at Tokyo Medical University. I live in a small apartment in Tokyo, but I want to move to the countryside someday and work in a hospital. I have two younger sisters. We all get along very well. I like to dance in my free time. I take ballet lessons, but I like flamenco dancing, too. I sometimes dance at festivals.

Sincerely,

Tomoko

a Circle the greeting and the closing.

b Draw a box around the sentence that tells Tomoko's age, nationality, and gender.

c What other topics does Tomoko talk about? Check (✓) them.

☐ her dislikes	☐ her friends	☐ her interests	☐ her school
☐ her family	☐ her future plans	☐ her job	☐ where she lives

d Tomoko used *Sincerely* for a closing. Check (✓) three other ways Tomoko could end her e-mail.

☐ Always,	☐ See you soon,	☐ Love,	☐ Thank you,	☐ Best regards,

2 Compare answers with a partner.

7 Write!

1 Choose someone to write an e-mail to and introduce yourself. Check (✓) one of the boxes below. You can also write your own idea.

☐ Your new pen pal   ☐ A new classmate

☐ Your future homestay hosts   ☐ _____
                                                          (your idea)

2 Now write your e-mail. Use your ideas from Part 5. Use the format below.

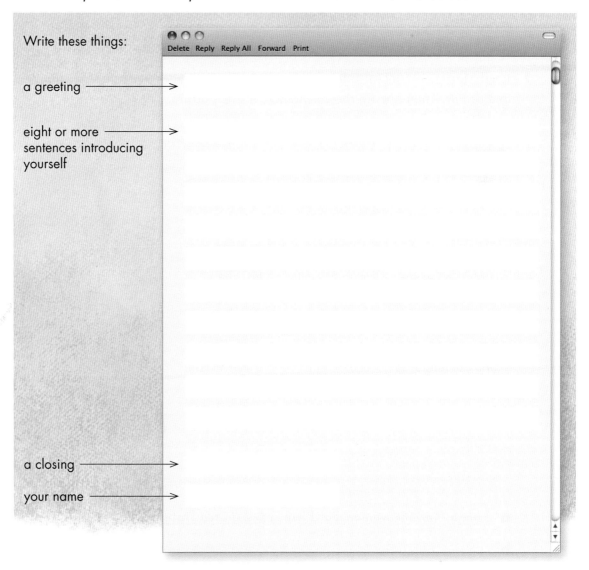

Write these things:

a greeting ⟶

eight or more sentences introducing yourself ⟶

a closing ⟶

your name ⟶

● ○ ○
Delete   Reply   Reply All   Forward   Print

In your journal . . .

Write about what you like to do in your free time.
Do you have a hobby or other special interests?

8 Editing

CONNECTING SENTENCES

You can use *and* or *but* to connect sentences. Put a comma (,) before *but*.

To connect sentences with similar or additional information, use *and*.

> I am Korean.
> I live in Seoul. → *I am Korean and I live in Seoul.*

To connect sentences with different or unexpected information, use *but*.

> I am Korean.
> I live in Sydney. → *I am Korean, but I live in Sydney.*

1 Read Marita's e-mail introducing herself. Mark the places to connect with *and* or *but*. Then rewrite these sentences at the bottom.

Delete Reply Reply All Forward Print

Hi Julie,

I will be your new roommate at Central Canadian College this fall, so let me tell you about myself. I am a Mexican woman. I live in the United States. I have traveled a lot. I have never been to Canada. I love science. I want to study biology in college. In my free time, I like listening to music. I like singing, too. Do you like music? What kind of music do you like? Please write back to me. Tell me something about yourself.

See you soon,
Marita

a *I am a Mexican woman, but I live in the United States.*

b _____

c _____

d _____

e _____

2 Now look at the e-mail you wrote in Part 7. See if you can improve your sentences.

9 Giving feedback

1 Exchange your revised e-mail with a partner. Read your partner's revised e-mail and follow the instructions below.

a Write your partner's greeting and closing.

_____   _____

b Did your partner include these things? Check (✓) the boxes.

	Yes	No
Name	☐	☐
Age	☐	☐
Gender	☐	☐
Nationality	☐	☐

c Write the topics your partner wrote about.

_____   _____

_____   _____

d Think of two more things you would like to know about your partner. Write two questions.

_____

_____

2 Write a short letter to your partner. Tell your partner about things you liked in the e-mail and ask questions. Then give the letter to your partner.

Dear Sung-Jae,
I like your e-mail. You said your English name is Jay. Who gave you that name?

Best regards,
Anna

3 Can any of your partner's comments help you make your e-mail better?

1 Write your address in English. Look at the examples. Then write your address below.

Bob Green	name	Linda Webb
2120 Forest Street, Apt. 2A	street address	14 Stamford Road
Honolulu, Hawaii 96811	city, state or province, and postal code	Oakhill
		Essex CM20 2JE
USA	country	UK

_____

_____

_____

_____

_____

2 When you write a letter, sign your name at the bottom in a special way with what is called a "signature." Practice writing your signature three times.

Signature   **Your signature**

Kana Kubota   _____
Kana Kubota

Michael Clark   _____
Michael Clark   _____

3 An e-mail signature is different. It is the information, symbols, or shapes you put at the bottom with your name. Make your own e-mail signature.

```
        ***   ***
         *     *
          **
         ****
- - - - - - - - - - - -
-        David Ko       -
-       dko@osu.edu     -
-   Ohio State University  -
-      1410 High Street   -
-     Columbus, OH 43210  -
-       (614) 292-1131    -
- - - - - - - - - - - -
```

An important place

1 Brainstorming

1 Label the picture with words from the box. Then compare answers with a partner.

- ☐ my friend's apartment
- ☐ a school
- ☐ a park
- ☐ a soccer field
- ☐ a river
- ☑ a store

a _____

b _____

c a store

d _____

e _____

f _____

2 What are some places that are important to you? What important or interesting things happened to you there? Brainstorm and make two lists.

Important place	What happened?
a park	I met my future wife

3 Compare lists with a partner. Can you add more places and events to your lists?

> **Later in this unit . . .**
>
> You will write about an important place and what happened to you there.
>
> You will also learn how to set the scene and write an ending to a personal story.

2 Analyzing a paragraph

1 Read the paragraph and follow the instructions below.

(1) There was a small playground near my home. (2) One day, when I was in the fourth grade, I took my little sister to the playground. (3) It was raining. (4) We played in the rain and had fun. (5) It was muddy, so we got very dirty. (6) When we got home, our parents were angry.

a Check (✓) the topic of the paragraph above.

☐ A beautiful place near my home
☐ Playing in a playground
☐ Angry parents

b Look at sentence 1 in the paragraph. Write a similar sentence with these words.

interesting shops / next to / my school

_____

_____

c Look at sentence 6 in the paragraph. Write a similar sentence with these words.

came to class late / teacher / upset

_____

_____

2 Compare answers with a partner.

Talk about it.

Tell your partner about a place where you liked to play as a child.

3 Learning about organization

1 Where are these places? Complete the sentences below with words from the Word File.

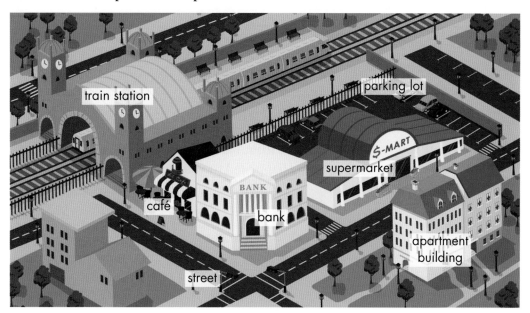

a There was a parking lot _____*behind*_____ the supermarket.

b There was a bank _____ the supermarket.

c There was a café _____ the bank and the train station.

d There was an apartment building _____ the supermarket.

Word File

☑ behind
☐ between
☐ in front of
☐ next to

2 When did this happen? Complete the sentences with words from the Word File.

There was a bank on the corner of 22nd Street. _____*When I was*_____ 21 years old, I got my first job in the office there. _____ to work, I carefully chose my clothes. I wore a dark blue suit.

_____ I arrived at the office, I looked around. No one else was wearing a suit. They were wearing jeans and T-shirts. I was so embarrassed! _____, I dressed differently.

Word File

☐ Before I went
☑ When I was
☐ After that
☐ As soon as

4 Working on content

1 Before you start writing, think about what you want to say. Write some
notes to help you. Read these notes that a student wrote about his
important place.

> <u>An important place</u>
>
> a park near my home
>
> <u>When did something important happen?</u>
>
> when I was a university student
>
> <u>What happened?</u>
>
> - I saw a beautiful woman
> - my friend introduced us
> - we started talking

2 Look again at your brainstorming list from Part 1. Choose a place where
something important or interesting happened to you. Write notes about
your important place.

> <u>An important place</u>
>
>
> <u>When did something important happen?</u>
>
>
> <u>What happened?</u>

3 Work in small groups. Take turns telling each other about your important
places. Ask questions like these:

- What is your important place? Where is it?
- When did something important happen there?
- What happened?

5 Learning more about organization

1 Look at the pictures. Complete the personal stories below with information from the box.

☐ my boss was angry with me   ☐ surprised, but happy
☑ we all cheered   ☐ proud
☐ my friend gave me a new one   ☐ embarrassed
☐ I lost the race   ☐ disappointed

a After my team got the trophy,

we all cheered _____!

We were _____.

b After I arrived late for my job,

_____.

I was _____.

c After I fell down,

_____.

I was _____.

d After I lost my favorite bracelet,

_____.

I was _____.

2 Now use your information from Part 4 to write an ending for your own story.

_____

_____

6 Analyzing a model

1 You are going to write about an important place and what happened there. First, read Tam's story and follow the instructions below.

Near my home in Bangkok, there was a beautiful park. One day, when I was a university student, I went there with my friends. We sat under a tree and watched people walk by. I saw a group of young women. One was so beautiful. My friend told me that she was his cousin. He introduced me to her. We talked for hours. I was a little nervous, but very excited. After that, I met her family. Three years ago, I got married to the beautiful woman I met in the park!

a Underline the sentence that tells what and where the special place was.

b Put a star (∗) above the phrases that tell when the story happened.

c Put a check (✓) above the words that join two sentences.

d Draw a box around the sentence that tells the writer's feelings.

e Circle the sentence that tells the outcome.

2 Compare answers with a partner.

7 Write!

1 Plan your paragraph about your important place and what happened there.

    a On a separate piece of paper, draw a simple picture or map of your important place.

    b Write one or two sentences to set the scene. Use your picture and what you wrote in Part 4 to help you.

    _____

    _____

    c Write two sentences for the ending. See if you can improve what you wrote in Part 5.

    _____

    _____

2 Now write a paragraph about an important place and what happened there. Use the sentences above to start and end the story.

In your journal . . .

Write about one of your favorite places. What do you do there? How often do you go there?

8 Editing

USING PREPOSITIONS

You can use *in*, *on*, and *at* to describe where things are.

Inside something:

I work in a restaurant in Seattle. It has a kitchen in the back.

On top of or touching:

It's on a hill on a small street. It's on the corner.

At a specific point or place:

It's at 236 Pine Street. I work at the front counter.

1 Complete the paragraph with prepositions from the box above.

When I was in high school, my family and I spent a year __in__ Canada.
We lived _____ 67 Prince Arthur Street _____ Montreal, Canada. There were
many cafés _____ Prince Arthur Street, so I went out for coffee. I found an
interesting French café _____ the corner, so I went _____. There were some
pictures of old Montreal _____ the walls. There were many people sitting
_____ the tables, and they all spoke French. I didn't know much French, so I
was nervous. I ordered a "café au lait" in French from the clerk standing
_____ the counter. That's a cup of coffee with milk _____ it. I also put some
money _____ the counter. The clerk said something, but I didn't understand.
"My French is bad!" I thought. Then she said it again: "Do you want it _____
a paper cup?" She spoke to me in English, not French! I was so embarrassed.

2 Now look at the paragraph you wrote in Part 7. See if you can improve your sentences.

18   Unit 2

9 Giving feedback

1 Exchange your revised paragraph with a partner. Read your partner's revised paragraph and follow the instructions below.

   a Answer these questions about your partner's paragraph.

   Where is the important place?

   _____

   When did something important happen there?

   _____

   What happened?

   _____

   What was the ending?

   _____

   b Circle the words that describe your partner's paragraph. You can also use your own words.

funny	interesting	sad
scary	_____	_____

2 Write a short letter to your partner. Write something you like and a question you have. Then give the letter to your partner.

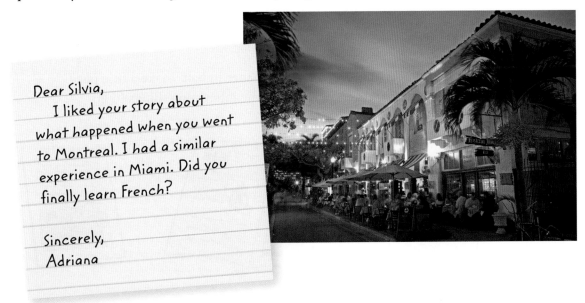

Dear Silvia,
   I liked your story about what happened when you went to Montreal. I had a similar experience in Miami. Did you finally learn French?

Sincerely,
Adriana

3 Can any of your partner's comments help you make your paragraph better?

JUST FOR FUN

1 Make a guidebook for newcomers: people who have just arrived in your city or town. Work in small groups. Decide whether you will make the guidebook for children, teenagers, or adults. Check (✓) your selection and write three interesting things to do.

☐ Children   ☐ Teenagers   ☐ Adults

visit the children's library   go to Riverside Park   spend time in the museum

a _____   a _____   a _____

b _____   b _____   b _____

c _____   c _____   c _____

2 Now write sentences like these using your information.

> *Visit the Children's Library! There are lots of fun things to do there. You can listen to stories, get help with homework, and play on the computers. You can also borrow books.*

3 To make your guidebook, fold a piece of paper in half. Make a title page. Use the other three pages to write about the interesting things to do. Include pictures and a map.

4 When you finish, share your newcomer's guidebook with your classmates.

An ideal partner

1 Brainstorming

1 What characteristics are important in an ideal partner? Check (✓) three.

☐ is good-looking   ☐ doesn't lie   ☐ cares about fashion

☐ is romantic   ☐ has a nice family   ☐ likes to travel

2 Brainstorm and make a list. Write five or more characteristics that are important to you.

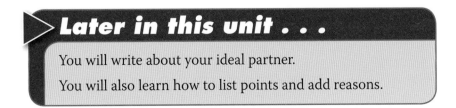

Characteristics of an ideal partner

likes to travel

3 Compare lists with a classmate. Can you add more characteristics to your list?

> ### Later in this unit . . .
> You will write about your ideal partner.
> You will also learn how to list points and add reasons.

2 Analyzing a paragraph

1 Read the paragraph and follow the instructions below.

(1) What kind of partner do I want? (2) First, I want a partner who is outgoing. (3) Second, I would like a partner who likes to travel because I like to go to new places. (4) Third, I prefer someone who can speak English well.

a Put a star (✱) above the three words that put the sentences in order.

b Underline the phrase that tells *why* the writer wants a partner who likes to travel.

c Look at sentence 2 in the paragraph. Write a similar sentence with these words.

First / partner / likes children

_____

_____

d Look at sentence 3 in the paragraph. Write a similar sentence with these words.

Second / go to concerts / I like music

_____

_____

2 Compare answers with a classmate.

Talk about it.

Tell a classmate if you would like an outgoing partner.

3 Working on content

1 You can get ideas to write about by interviewing others. Read the example interview.

Do you prefer a partner who is playful or serious?

I prefer a partner who is serious.

2 Interview a classmate. Ask each other which characteristics are important in an ideal partner. Then check (✓) *your* answers in the chart.

Do you prefer a partner who . . . ?

		not sure or don't care	
a	is playful ☐	☐	☐ is serious
b	is talkative ☐	☐	☐ is quiet
c	is good-looking ☐	☐	☐ has a great personality
d	likes to go out ☐	☐	☐ likes to stay home
e	is adventurous ☐	☐	☐ is careful
f	is passionate ☐	☐	☐ is calm
g	likes to do things alone ☐	☐	☐ doesn't like to do things alone
h	thinks money is important ☐	☐	☐ doesn't think money is important
i	likes change ☐	☐	☐ doesn't like change
j	thinks family is important ☐	☐	☐ thinks friends are important

3 Now ask, "What are three other characteristics you want in an ideal partner?" Then complete the sentence with *your* answers.

I want a partner who _____,

_____,

and _____.

4 Learning about organization

Use words like *First, Second, Third, Next,* and *Finally* to list the points
that explain the main idea.

> *What kind of partner do I want? He*
> *should be warm. He should be outgoing.*
> *He should have lots of friends.*

→

> *What kind of partner do I want? First,*
> *he should be warm. Second, he should be*
> *outgoing. He should have lots of friends.*

1 Read the sentences. Then write *First, Second,* and *Third* in the
correct places.

First,

What kind of partner do I want? I want

a partner who likes movies. I would like a

partner who likes to dance. I love music

and dancing. I would like a partner who

thinks family is important. My family is

important to me.

2 Write the three most important characteristics for your ideal partner from
the interview in Part 3. Then complete the sentence about each one.

Qualities	Sentences
a _____	I want _____.
b _____	I would like _____.
c _____	I prefer _____.

3 Now rewrite these sentences with words like *First* and *Second*.

_____

_____

_____

5 Learning more about organization

ADDING REASONS

Add reasons to your writing. Use *because*.

> *I want a partner who is tall.*
> *I am tall.*
> →
> *I want a partner who is tall*
> *because I am tall.*

1 Rewrite these sentences using *because*. You can use the reasons below or change them to something else.

a I would like a partner who is serious about school.
I like people with a good education.

_____

_____

_____

b I prefer a partner who likes sports. I play tennis a lot.

_____

_____

_____

c I want a partner who doesn't tell lies. I had a partner once who lied to me and hurt my feelings.

_____

_____

d I want a partner who likes children. I want to have a big family.

_____

_____

2 Write reasons for the three characteristics you wrote about in Part 4. Add reasons with *because*.

a _____

_____

b _____

_____

c _____

_____

6 Analyzing a model

1 You are going to write about your ideal partner. First, read Emily's paragraph and follow the instructions below.

> *
>   What kind of partner do I want? First, I want a partner who likes sports because I like to be active. Sports are an important part of my life. I'd rather play tennis or jog than stay at home and watch TV all day. Second, I would like a partner who likes being with groups of people because I enjoy meeting people. I learn interesting things when I talk to others. Third, I would like a partner who likes to travel. I love to travel, and it is my dream to live abroad. Also, if my partner and I both like to travel, we can learn about different cultures together.

a Put a star (✱) above the words that put Emily's ideas in order.

b Write the three characteristics Emily's partner should have.

_____   _____   _____

c Write three more phrases Emily uses to write about what she likes or wants.

- ■ I want   ■ _____
- ■ I like   ■ _____
- ■ I'd rather   ■ _____

2 Compare answers with a classmate.

7 Write!

1 Plan your paragraph about your ideal partner.

a Use the first sentence of the model in Part 2.

_____

b Write three characteristics you want in your partner (look at Part 3).

_____

c Write three reasons to support the characteristics you chose (look at Part 5).

▪ _____

_____

▪ _____

_____

▪ _____

_____

2 Now write your paragraph about your ideal partner. Use paragraph format.

In your journal . . .

Write a story about an ideal day with your ideal partner.

8 Editing

1 Read the paragraph. Circle the sentences that you can combine.

First, I want a partner who does water sports. (I like swimming. I also
like sailing. I also like surfing.) Second, I want a partner who prefers
staying home at night. I don't like going out. I prefer staying at home with
my partner. I prefer being alone with my partner. I like watching TV with
my partner. I also like listening to music with my partner. Third, I hope my
partner is a good listener. I hope my partner can understand my problems.
I also hope my partner can give me advice. I like people who think about
life's problems. I like people who discuss such problems.

2 Combine the sentences you circled with *and*. Make them as short
as possible.

a *I like swimming, sailing, and surfing.*

b _____

c _____

d _____

e _____

3 Now look at the paragraph you wrote in Part 7. See if you can improve your sentences.

9 Giving feedback

1 Exchange your revised paragraph with a classmate. Read your classmate's revised paragraph and follow the instructions below.

   a Check (✓) the sentences that are true.

      ☐ The paragraph begins with *What kind of partner do I want?*
      ☐ There are three characteristics of an ideal partner.
      ☐ The three characteristics are marked with words like *First, Second,* and *Third.*
      ☐ There is a reason for each characteristic.

   b Write the three characteristics your classmate wrote about.

   _____   _____   _____

   c Look at the pictures. Check (✓) an ideal partner for your classmate, or make a new one.

☐ **pro tennis player**

loves parties

☐ **artist**

interesting ideas

☐ **college professor**

reads every night

☐ **company president**

loves to work

☐ _____
(your idea)
_____

2 Write a short letter to your classmate. Write your ideas or questions about his or her writing. Then give the letter to your classmate.

3 Can any of your classmate's comments help you make your paragraph better?

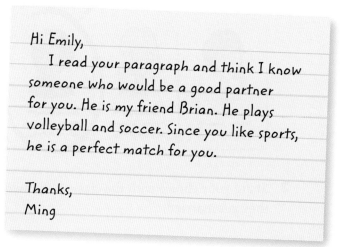

Hi Emily,
   I read your paragraph and think I know someone who would be a good partner for you. He is my friend Brian. He plays volleyball and soccer. Since you like sports, he is a perfect match for you.

Thanks,
Ming

JUST FOR FUN

1 Make up characters to take part in a matchmaking* game. Half of the class
will make up male characters and half will make up female characters.
Work alone or with a classmate and follow the instructions below.

a On a separate piece of paper, write a
name for your character.

b Draw his or her picture.

c Write your character's information:
name, age, gender, nationality, job,
special talents, etc.

d Write at least four characteristics that
describe your character. Use ideas
from Part 3 or your own ideas.

Name: _____

Information: _____

_____

_____

Characteristics: _____

_____

_____

2 Now play the matchmaking game.

a Put the male and female
characters in rows across
from each other.

b Read the description of your
character out loud. Your
classmates will ask questions
about your character.

c Listen to all the descriptions
of the other characters. Then
write down the name of the
character that is the best
partner for yours.

3 Share your choice with the class. If the two characters choose each other,
they get married!

* Matchmaking means to find a husband or wife for someone else.

My favorite photo

1 Brainstorming

1 Look at these photos. Do you have any photos like these? Check (✓) them.

☐ my friends and me   ☐ my grandparents   ☐ my wedding

☐ a sports team I was on   ☐ my graduation   ☐ me as a child

2 What are some other photos you have? Brainstorm and make a list.

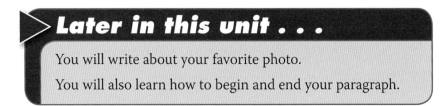

My photos

a trip to China
my co-workers and my workplace
my cousin

3 Compare lists with a partner. Can you add more photos to your list?

> **Later in this unit . . .**
>
> You will write about your favorite photo.
>
> You will also learn how to begin and end your paragraph.

2 Analyzing a paragraph

1 Read the paragraph and follow the instructions below.

(1) My favorite photo is of my friends and me on my twenty-first birthday. (2) It was taken last year at a restaurant. (3) My friends gave me some cards and presents and sang "Happy Birthday." (4) I like this photo because it reminds me of a very special day.

a Put a star (✱) above the phrases that tell *who* is in the photo and *when* it was taken.

b Underline the sentence that tells *why* this photo is important to the writer.

c Look at sentence 1 in the paragraph. Write a similar sentence with these words.

my family and me / New Year's Day

_____

_____

d Look at sentence 2 in the paragraph. Write a similar sentence with these words.

when I was sixteen / my grandmother's house

_____

_____

2 Compare answers with a partner.

Talk about it.

Tell your partner about a photo of you from a birthday party.

3 Working on content

1 When you write, think about *who*, *what*, *when*, and *where*. Look at Wes's chart about his photo on page 36.

Wes's photo	
Who my grandparents	**What** She fell in the water. She couldn't swim. He rescued her. They fell in love that day. They got married a few months later.
When the day after they met 1950	**Where** It was in Brooklyn, New York.

2 Look at your brainstorming list from Part 1. Choose one of your favorite photos to write about. Then complete the chart for your photo.

Your photo	
Who	**What**
When	**Where**

3 Show your chart to a partner. Your partner will ask questions. Is there anything you want to change in your chart? Is there anything you want to add to it?

4 Learning about organization

When you write about your photo, begin by giving background information about it. You can include these details:

- who or what is in the photo (use *is, are*)
- when the photo was taken (use *was*)
- where the photo was taken (use *was*)

1 Read the background information about different photos and follow the instructions.

Who or what?

My favorite photo is of my soccer team and me.

a Write a sentence about the people or things in your photo.

_____

_____

When?

My favorite photo was taken three years ago on the day that I got a special award.

b Write a sentence about when your photo was taken.

_____

_____

Where?

My favorite photo was taken at Marine World.

c Write a sentence about where your photo was taken.

_____

_____

5 Learning more about organization

WRITING A CONCLUDING SENTENCE

A concluding sentence ends a paragraph. In a paragraph about a photo, the concluding sentence often tells why the photo is important to the writer.

A special person: *I like the photo because it is of my best friend.*

A special time or place: *This photo reminds me of my high school days.*

An event: *This photo helps me remember my wedding dinner.*

1 Read the groups of sentences. Check (✓) the best concluding sentence in each group.

a ☐ The Grand Canyon is in Arizona. ☐ I like this photo because our trip to the Grand Canyon was wonderful. ☐ It took us six hours to hike up the trail.	**b** ☐ My friend, John, took this photo during my winter vacation. ☐ After we went inside, we had some tea. ☐ This photo reminds me of the trips I took with that good friend.
c ☐ When I look at this photo, I remember our wonderful concert. ☐ I'm glad I didn't forget the words to the songs. ☐ I was very nervous, but I sang well.	**d** ☐ This photo reminds me of many things. ☐ I took this photo the day I visited a Japanese castle. ☐ This photo helps me remember the years I lived in Japan.

2 Now write a concluding sentence for the photo you chose in Part 3.

6 Analyzing a model

1 You are going to write about your favorite photo. First, read about Wes's photo and follow the instructions below.

My favorite photo is of my grandparents on the day after they met. It was taken in 1950 at the beach in Brooklyn, New York. The day before, my grandfather rescued my grandmother. She went into the ocean, and she fell. The water was deep, and she couldn't swim. My grandfather went into the water and saved her. He brought her to the shore. I think that was also when they fell in love. A few months later, they got married. This photo is special to me because it helps me remember my grandparents. It also reminds me of how happy their marriage was.

a Underline the two sentences that give background information.

b Circle the concluding sentences that tell why the photo is important to Wes.

c Put a box around the sentences that tell what happened on the day the photo was taken.

2 Compare answers with a partner.

7 Write!

1 Plan your paragraph about your favorite photo.

    a First, put a photocopy of the photo at the top of your paper, or make a simple line drawing to show what the photo looks like.

    b Include background information about your photo.

    _____

    c Explain what happened and give additional details (use your chart from Part 3).

    _____
    _____
    _____
    _____

    d Write a concluding sentence that tells why the photo is important to you.

    _____
    _____

2 Now write your paragraph about your favorite photo.

In your journal . . .

Write about taking photos. Do you like taking photos? What kinds of photos do you take?

8 Editing

MIXING PAST AND PRESENT TENSE

When you write about what happened in the photo, use the past tense.

I was afraid to get into the pool. My mother had to help me.

When you write about the photo itself, use the present tense.

Background information: *My favorite photo is of me at my first swimming lesson.*

Concluding sentence: *The photo reminds me of that scary day.*

1 Complete the paragraph. Use the correct verb tenses.

     My favorite photo is of Kailua Beach in Hawaii. It was taken about five years

ago. The photo _____*shows*_____ (show) the beach in front and the beautiful blue

ocean in the back. I _____ (be) not in the photo because I

_____ (take) it. I _____ (go) to Kailua Beach by bicycle. I

_____ (rent) a bicycle in Waikiki and _____ (ride) it to Kailua.

It _____ (be) a very long and dangerous ride. Many trucks and cars

quickly _____ (drive) past me, and sometimes they _____ (are)

very close. I also _____ (have) to ride over a mountain. I

_____ (get) so tired, but when I _____ (arrive) at Kailua Beach,

I _____ (see) this beautiful view. It _____ (touch) my heart and

_____ (bring) tears to my eyes. This photo _____ (be) so

simple, but it _____ (be) my treasure. I _____ (love) it because

it _____ (help) me remember that wonderful day.

2 Now look at the paragraph you wrote in Part 7. See if you can improve your sentences.

9 Giving feedback

1 Exchange your revised paragraph with a partner. Read your partner's revised paragraph and follow the instructions below.

a Circle the words that best describe your partner's photo. You can also use your own words.

beautiful	exciting	interesting	unusual	_____
cute	funny	strange	warm	_____

b Does your partner's paragraph answer these questions? Check (✓) Yes or No.

	Yes	No
Who is in the photo?	☐	☐
What happened that day?	☐	☐
When was the photo taken?	☐	☐
Where did this event happen?	☐	☐
Why is the photo important to the writer?	☐	☐

2 Write a short letter to your partner. Write something you like and a question you have. Then give the letter to your partner.

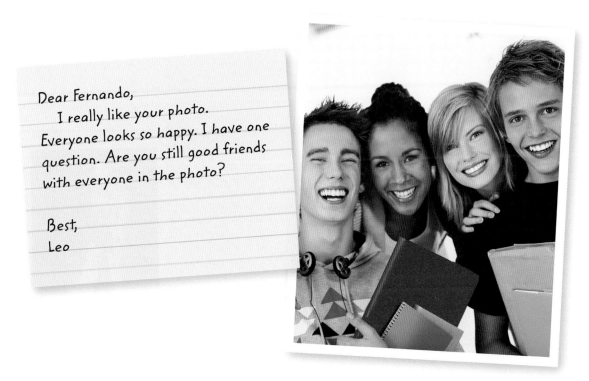

Dear Fernando,
I really like your photo. Everyone looks so happy. I have one question. Are you still good friends with everyone in the photo?

Best,
Leo

3 Can any of your partner's comments help you make your paragraph better?

1   Make a photo time line of your life. Look at the example.

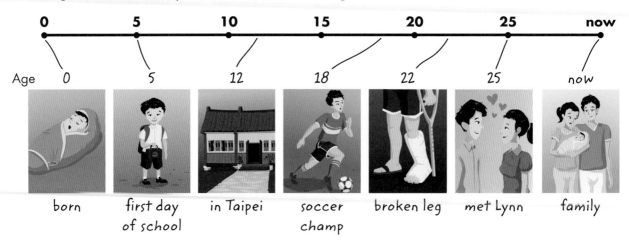

0	5	10	15	20	25	now

Age   0   5   12   18   22   25   now

born   first day   in Taipei   soccer   broken leg   met Lynn   family
          of school   champ

2   Write five important life experiences in the chart. Write how old you were.
       Include what you are doing now, too.

Important experiences	Your age
▪ I was born.	▪ 0 years old
▪	▪
▪	▪
▪	▪
▪	▪
▪	▪
▪	▪

3   Use a big piece of paper. Draw a picture or
       put a photo of each event on a time line.
       Write your age for each.

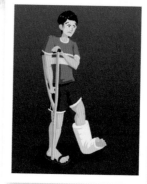

4   Below each photo, write a title and the story
       about what happened. Look at this example.

5   Share your time line with your class.
       What new things did you learn about
       your classmates?

Broken Leg

I had a bicycle accident just before a
soccer match. I was at home for a week,
and all my friends came to visit me. I could
not play soccer for the rest of that year.

My seal

1 Brainstorming

1 Here is a seal from an international college. What does each symbol on the seal represent? Complete the sentences with words and phrases from the box.

> ☐ sports ☐ people from many cultures
> ☑ strength ☐ study

a The tiger represents _____strength_____.

b The books represent _____.

c The ball and racket represent _____.

d The hands represent _____.

2 Think of words and phrases that describe you. Brainstorm and make four lists.

My favorite activities	My experiences	My personality	My favorite people
surfing	trip to Paris	friendly	Bob, my best friend

3 Compare lists with a partner. Can you add more words and phrases to your lists?

> ### ▶ Later in this unit . . .
> You will design and write about your own seal.
>
> You will also learn how to organize information by location and write topic sentences.

2 Analyzing a paragraph

1 Read the paragraph and follow the instructions below.

(1) My seal has two symbols: a guitar and four stars. (2) There is a guitar in the center of my seal. (3) The guitar represents my hobby, playing pop music. (4) There are four stars above the guitar. (5) They represent my four best friends.

a Write the two symbols for the seal above. Then write what the symbols represent.

Symbols	What the symbols represent
_____	_____
_____	_____

b Look at sentence 1 in the paragraph. Write a similar sentence with these words.

seal / three symbols / pen, a rose, and two hearts

_____

_____

c Look at sentence 3 in the paragraph. Write a similar sentence with these words.

pen / my dream / becoming a writer

_____

_____

d Look at sentence 5 in the paragraph. Write a similar sentence with these words.

The rose and two hearts / wife and our two children

_____

_____

2 Compare answers with a partner.

Talk about it.

Tell your partner about a special interest or hobby.

3 Working on content

1 A symbol is one thing that represents something else. A plant or animal is a good symbol for someone's personality or character. A symbol can also show what you want to be or your ideal character. Look at this chart that a student completed about the symbols that he chose.

Plant or animal		Reasons
a plant: a cactus		1 A cactus is strong. 2 A cactus can live without water.
an animal: a puppy		1 A puppy is playful. 2 A puppy is friendly to everyone.

2 Which plant or animal best represents your character or ideal character? Why? Complete the chart for yourself.

Plant or animal	Reasons
_____	1 _____
	2 _____

3 Now interview a partner. Why did your partner choose that plant or animal? Follow the example.

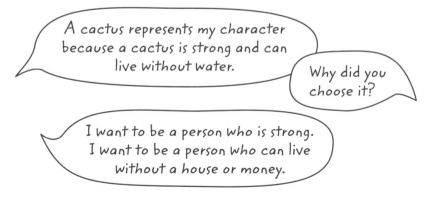

A cactus represents my character because a cactus is strong and can live without water.

Why did you choose it?

I want to be a person who is strong. I want to be a person who can live without a house or money.

4 Use sentences from your interview to explain your plant or animal and why it represents you. Follow the example.

A cactus represents my ideal character because . . .

4 Learning about organization

Write about the symbol in the center of your seal first. Then write about the other symbols and their locations. Here are useful words for writing about where each part is.

above
↑
on / to the left of ⟵ in the center ⟶ on / to the right of
↓
below

1 Look at Ruby's seal and then design your own. Follow the instructions.

a Choose the plant or animal from Part 3 for the center of your seal. Draw it on your seal.

b Think of at least two other things to represent you. (Look at your brainstorming list in Part 1.) Draw the symbols for them in your seal.

Ruby's Seal

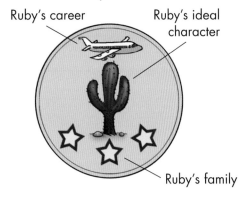

Ruby's career   Ruby's ideal character

Ruby's family

2 Look at Ruby's seal. Where are the symbols? Complete the sentences.

a There is a cactus _____ of Ruby's seal.

b _____ the cactus there are stars.

c There is a plane _____ the cactus.

3 Where are the symbols on your seal? Write sentences.

a _____

b _____

c _____

5 Learning more about organization

TOPIC SENTENCES

A topic sentence is useful for organizing a paragraph. It tells what the paragraph is about, or the main idea. It is like a summary of the paragraph.

Topic sentence: *The apple is a symbol of many things.*

1 These sentences come from a paragraph about symbols. Complete the sentences with words from the box.

☐ the royal family   ☐ a hospital   ☐ knowledge   ☐ good luck   ☑ the Queen

In England, a red rose represents ____the Queen____. In Germany, an

apple represents _____. In Japan, a chrysanthemum

represents _____. In the United States, an H **H** represents

_____. In China, the number eight **8** represents _____.

2 Now check (✓) the best topic sentence for this paragraph.

☐ Flowers represent the rulers of countries.
☐ There are many different symbols around the world.
☐ The red rose is the most beautiful symbol.

3 Check (✓) the best topic sentence for a paragraph about Ruby's seal in Part 4.

☐ I am going to write about my seal.
☐ The cactus is my favorite symbol.
☐ My seal has three symbols: a cactus, stars, and an airplane.

4 Now write a topic sentence for a paragraph about your seal.

_____

6 Analyzing a model

1 You are going to write about your personal seal. First, read about Manuel's seal and follow the instructions below.

    My seal has four symbols: a pine tree, wheels, a sun, and snow. The pine tree is in the center. It represents my ideal character because a pine tree is always green and never changes. I want to be a person who doesn't change easily. Below the tree there are wheels. The wheels represent my motorcycle. Above the tree on the right there is a sun, and on the left there is snow. The sun represents Costa Rica, where I was born. It's warm and sunny there. The snow represents Canada, where I live now. It's cold and snowy there. I think both countries have shaped my character.

a Underline the topic sentence.

b Put a star (✱) above the phrases that tell where the symbols on the seal are located.

c Write the four symbols and what they represent.

	Symbols	What the symbols represent
Symbol 1:	_pine tree_	_a character that never changes_
Symbol 2:	_____	_____
Symbol 3:	_____	_____
Symbol 4:	_____	_____

2 Compare answers with a partner.

7 Write!

1 Plan your paragraph about your personal seal.

    a Draw the seal at the top of your paper.

    b Write a topic sentence.

_____

    c Describe where each symbol is.

_____

_____

    d Write a description of the main symbol in the center: a plant or animal.

_____

_____

    e Explain what each symbol represents.

_____

_____

2 Now write a paragraph about your personal seal.

In your journal . . .

Write about another seal that you've seen. Where did you see it? What did it look like? What do you think the symbols represent?

8 Editing

COMMAS WITH *BECAUSE*

In Unit 3, you learned to connect sentences with *because* to give reasons.

> *A pine tree represents my ideal character because it is always green and never changes.*

Because can also come at the beginning of a sentence. Look at how a comma is used.

> *Because a pine tree is always green and never changes, it represents my ideal character.*

1 Match each symbol to a reason. Draw lines.

Symbol	Reason
a my seal has three musical notes on it	I often have to travel for work
b there is a piano in the center of my seal	I am small and strong
c I used an ant to represent myself	my hobby is sailing
d the main color of my seal is green	music is the most important thing in my life
e I put ocean waves at the bottom	I love singing
f the airplane ticket represents my job	I love trees

2 Write sentences that start with *because*. Use the symbols and the reasons from Step 1.

    a *Because I love singing, my seal has three musical notes on it.*

    b _____

    c _____

    d _____

    e _____

    f _____

3 Now look at the paragraph you wrote in Part 7. See if you can improve your sentences.

9 Giving feedback

1 Work in groups of four. Exchange your revised paragraph and the drawing of your seal with members of another group. Read all of the other group's revised paragraphs and complete the chart.

Which seal . . .	
surprised you the most?	_____
had the most interesting design?	_____
had the most unusual symbol?	_____
was easiest to understand?	_____

2 Each member should take one paragraph to give feedback on. Write the symbols and what they represent.

Group member's name: _____

Symbols	**What the symbols represent**
a _____	_____
b _____	_____
c _____	_____

3 Check (✓) the sentences that describe this paragraph.

☐ The paragraph has a topic sentence.

☐ There is a plant or animal in the seal.

☐ The paragraph explains where the symbols are.

☐ The symbols are explained clearly.

☐ The ideas are interesting.

☐ The paragraph needs more explanation.

4 Write a short letter to your classmate. Write something you like and a question you have. Then give the letter to your classmate.

> Dear Catherine,
> I liked your seal. I think an eagle is a good symbol for you. I liked the river, too, but I don't understand why the river was above the eagle. Can you tell me? Thank you.
>
> Your classmate,
> Eva

5 Can any of your classmate's comments help you make your paragraph better?

JUST FOR FUN

1 Make a group flag. Work in small groups. Choose a club or class as the subject for your flag. Circle your group's choice or write your own idea.

| English class | a club | science class | a sports team | _____ |

2 Choose two words from the Word File to represent your club or class. You can also use your own words. Then create a symbol for each word.

Words	Symbols

Word File

athletic	friendly
caring	hardworking
competitive	helpful
creative	modern
dependable	traditional

3 Decide on colors and symbols to represent your club or class. Finish the chart.

Color or symbol	What it represents

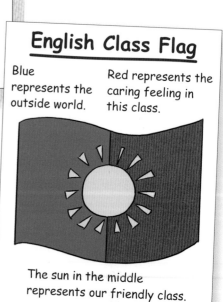

English Class Flag

Blue represents the outside world.

Red represents the caring feeling in this class.

The sun in the middle represents our friendly class.

4 Now make a poster. Draw the flag in the middle of a big piece of paper. Write an explanation for each part.

5 Present your poster to the class.

Party time

1 Brainstorming

1 Which of these activities would you like to do with your class? Check (✓) them.

☐ do a traditional dance   ☐ go on a hike   ☐ go to a museum

☐ have a pizza party   ☐ wear Hawaiian shirts   ☐ watch a movie

2 What other activities would you like to do with your class? Brainstorm and make a list.

<u>Class activities</u>

have a karaoke party

3 Compare lists with a partner. Can you add more activities to your list?

> ## Later in this unit . . .
>
> You will plan a class party and write a paragraph about it.
>
> You will also learn how to explain plans and give instructions.

2 Analyzing a paragraph

1 Read the paragraph and follow the instructions below.

(1) The end of the school year is coming, so let's go on a class hike! (2) The hike will start at 8:00 a.m. and end at 2:00 p.m. (3) Please be on time. (4) Bring shorts and a T-shirt because it will probably get hot in the afternoon.

a Put a star (✱) above the kind of class activity this paragraph is about.

b Read the sentences. Check (✓) two sentences to add to the paragraph.

☐ Don't forget to bring a water bottle.
☐ Hiking is less popular than snowboarding.
☐ We won't eat dinner there.
☐ We'll meet at Bell School at 6:50 a.m.

c Look at sentence 1 in the paragraph. Write a similar sentence with these words.

Winter is coming / class ski trip

_____

_____

d Look at sentence 4 in the paragraph. Write a similar sentence with these words.

Wear / coat and gloves / be cold

_____

_____

2 Compare answers with a partner.

Talk about it.

Tell your partner about a class trip you went on.

3 Working on content

1 Make notes to help you think of details to use in your writing. Look at Andy's notes about a class party. Then put these details in his party announcement below.

> "Aloha Friday" party on June 1
> in English class   Free!
> Questions, ask Andy
> Let's start at 11:00 a.m. and end at 12:10 p.m.

Class Party!

Date: _____

Starting time: _____

Cost per person: _____

Contact person: _____

Location: _____

Ending time: _____

2 Look again at your brainstorming list from Part 1. Choose an idea for a class party. Then complete the party announcement with party details.

Class Party!

Date: _____

Starting time: _____

Cost per person: _____

Contact person: _____

Location: _____

Ending time: _____

3 Read these topic sentences. Then write a similar topic sentence for a paragraph about your class party.

Summer is coming, so let's celebrate with an "Aloha Friday" party!

Let's have a karaoke party before final exams!

My topic sentence: _____

4 Learning about organization

Explain the plans for your party first, and then give instructions for each plan.
We use different kinds of sentences to explain plans and give instructions.

Plans	Instructions based on the plans
We will go to the Sunshine Theater.	*Please be on time.*
Then we will listen to music.	*Bring your favorite CD.*
After that, I will play the piano.	*Please learn the words to the song.*

1 Look at the pictures. Then complete the sentences about plans for a class
hiking party.

a We will meet at _____Bell School_____ at 6:50 a.m.

b Then we will take a _____ to
Riverview Park.

c After we get there, we will _____
along the trail to Crystal Pond.

d At Crystal Pond, we will _____.

2 Complete the instructions with words from the Word File. Then match the
letter of the plans in Step 1 with the instructions.

___d___ ___Bring___ something to eat and drink.

_____ Please do not _____ late.

_____ _____ old clothes because you will get dirty.

_____ Please _____ a bus ticket by Tuesday.

Word File

- ☑ to bring
- ☐ to arrive
- ☐ to buy
- ☐ to wear

5 Working more on content

1 One way to get ideas for your paragraph is to make a list of ideas. Write key words and phrases instead of sentences. Look at Andy's list of ideas for his party.

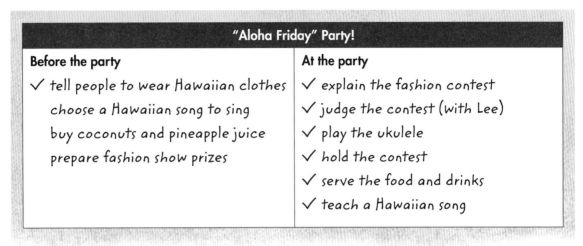

"Aloha Friday" Party!	
Before the party	**At the party**
✓ tell people to wear Hawaiian clothes choose a Hawaiian song to sing buy coconuts and pineapple juice prepare fashion show prizes	✓ explain the fashion contest ✓ judge the contest (with Lee) ✓ play the ukulele ✓ hold the contest ✓ serve the food and drinks ✓ teach a Hawaiian song

2 Now make a list of ideas for your party.

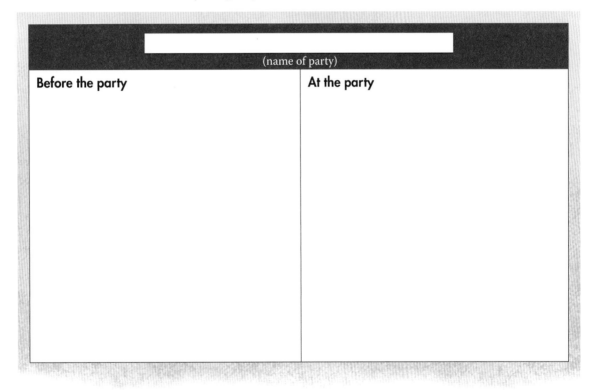

(name of party)	
Before the party	**At the party**

3 Look again at Andy's list. Notice he checked (✓) the information he wanted to include in his paragraph about the party. Look again at your list and check (✓) the information you want to include in your paragraph.

4 Show your list to a partner. Is there anything you need to change or add?

6 Analyzing a model

ALOHA Friday

1 You are going to write a party announcement and a paragraph about the party. First, read Andy's party announcement and paragraph and follow the instructions below.

"Aloha Friday" Party

Date: June 1

Location: English class

Cost per person: It's free!

Starting Time: 11:00 a.m.

Ending Time: 12:10 p.m.

Contact person: Andy

Summer is coming, so let's celebrate with an "Aloha Friday" party! Please wear Hawaiian clothes to the party because we are going to have a Hawaiian fashion contest. The Hawaiian clothes can be a Hawaiian shirt, a dress with a tropical print, or even sandals and a straw hat. At the beginning of class, each person will walk in front of the room so that we can choose the best Hawaiian look. After the contest, we will eat some coconuts and drink pineapple juice. I'll also play my ukulele and teach the class a Hawaiian song. Be there!

a Underline the topic sentence.

b Put a star (✷) above the phrases that explain the party plan.

c Circle the two sentences that give instructions.

d Draw a box around the sentence that gives examples of Hawaiian clothes.

2 Compare answers with a partner.

7 Write!

1 Plan the party announcement and paragraph for your party.

a Write these things for your notice.

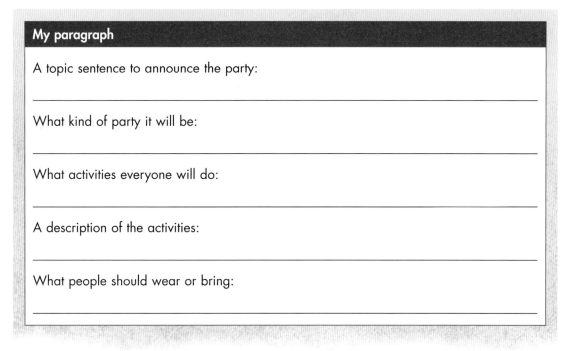

Class party announcement
The name of the party: _____
The day and time: _____
The place: _____
The contact person: _____
The cost: _____

b Remember to write these things for your paragraph.

My paragraph
A topic sentence to announce the party:
_____
What kind of party it will be:
_____
What activities everyone will do:
_____
A description of the activities:
_____
What people should wear or bring:
_____

2 Now write your party announcement and paragraph.

> ### In your journal . . .
> Write about the best party you have ever gone to. What kind of party was it? Where was it? What did you do at the party? Who came? What interesting things happened?

8 Editing

1   Rewrite the sentences two ways. Use *so that* and *to*.

a I will go to the restaurant tomorrow. I can make reservations for
our party.

(so that) _____

(to) _____

b Let's swap lunches on Tuesday. We can see what other people like to eat.

(so that) _____

(to) _____

c I think we should go to the movie early. We can buy popcorn and drinks
for everyone.

(so that) _____

(to) _____

d Let's meet at 6:15. We can get to the concert before it starts.

(so that) _____

(to) _____

e Bring some money. You can rent a boat at the lake.

(so that) _____

(to) _____

f Please bring a hat. You can keep from getting a sunburn.

(so that) _____

(to) _____

2   Now look at the party paragraph you wrote in Part 7. See if you can improve
your sentences.

9 Giving feedback

1 Exchange your revised paragraph with a partner. Read your partner's revised paragraph and follow the instructions below.

   a Did your partner answer these questions? Check (✓) the boxes.

	Yes	No
When and where will the party be?	☐	☐
How much will the party cost?	☐	☐
What kind of party will it be?	☐	☐
What activities will everyone do?	☐	☐
What should everyone wear or bring?	☐	☐

   b Circle one or two sentences that describe your partner's party. You can write your own sentences.

It's fun.	It's easy to do.	_____
It's unique.	It's free.	_____

2 Write a short letter to your partner. Write something you like and a question you have. Then give the letter to your partner.

Dear Andy,
   I liked your idea for an "Aloha Friday" party. I think it will be fun. I have some Hawaiian leis at home. Would you like me to bring them to the party? I can't wait for "Aloha Friday"!

Cheri

3 Can any of your partner's comments help you make your paragraph better?

4 Put all of the party ideas on desks. Then choose three parties you would like to attend and write them here.

   _____   _____   _____

5 Vote on a class party and do it!

1 Design a poster for your party. Follow the instructions.

a Choose a word from the box or your own word that explains the mood of your party. Write it on the line below.

crazy	elegant	exciting	exotic	friendly	quiet	traditional	unique

_____

b Read these design ideas. Then choose design ideas to use in your poster.

Color: Use colors and shapes to show the theme of your party.

White space: Leave some parts empty to make your design seem light.

Simplicity: To make your message powerful, don't put too many pictures in your poster.

Size: Make the most important information large and other information small.

2 Now design your poster.

Come to ALOHA Friday!

Summer is coming. We are celebrating with an Aloha Friday party. We are going to have a Hawaiian fashion contest and Hawaiian snacks. We will listen to ukulele music and learn a Hawaiian song. Get dressed in your best island fashions and enjoy the party!

Date: June 1   **Starting time:** 11:00 a.m.   **Contact Person:** Andy
Location: English class   **Ending time:** 12:10 p.m.   **Cost per person:** It's free!

If you have any questions, call Andy at 212-555-ANDY.

3 When you finish, hang your posters up around the classroom. Which posters have the best design?

Thank-you note

1 Brainstorming

1 Which of these nice things has someone done for you recently? Check (✓) them.

☐ listened to my problem ☐ gave me advice ☐ taught me how to drive

☐ made dinner for me ☐ lent me a cell phone ☐ gave me a present

2 Who has done something nice for you recently? Brainstorm and make two lists.

Who?	Did what?
my friend	drove me to work

3 Compare lists with a partner. Can you add more to your lists?

> **Later in this unit . . .**
>
> You will write a thank-you note expressing appreciation.
> You will also learn how to give reasons and use time markers.

2 Analyzing a paragraph

1 Read the paragraph and follow the instructions below.

(1) I want to thank you for giving me such a lovely gift. (2) I am sometimes late, so a clock is a perfect gift for me! (3) Also, it is just the right size for my desk. (4) Again, thanks so much for the gift.

a Underline the sentence that explains *why* this person is writing.

b Put a star (✱) above the phrases that describe *why* it is a good gift.

c Look at sentence 1 in the paragraph. Write a similar sentence with these words.

thank you / taking me / concert

_____

_____

d Look at sentence 4 in the paragraph. Write a similar sentence with these words.

thank you / an enjoyable evening

_____

_____

2 Compare answers with a partner.

Talk about it.

Tell your partner about a gift you received recently.

3 Learning about organization

Start your thank-you note with a reason for thanking someone. Use *for* + verb + *-ing* to give the reason.

Gio, I want to thank you. You helped me with my homework.	→	*Gio, I want to thank you for helping me with my homework.*
Rachel, I want to thank you. You came over and talked to me after I got some bad news.	→	*Rachel, I want to thank you for coming over and talking to me after I got some bad news.*

1 Rewrite these sentences. Use *for* + verb + *-ing*.

a I want to thank you. You helped me carry those heavy boxes.

_____

b I want to thank you. You showed me where the hospital is.

_____

c I want to thank you. You invited me to sit with you in the cafeteria.

_____

d I want to thank you. You taught me how to use my new cell phone.

_____

2 Now thank three classmates for something nice they did. Write their names. Then complete the sentences. Use *for* + verb + *-ing*.

a Classmate: _____. I want to thank you _____.

b Classmate: _____. I want to thank you _____.

c Classmate: _____. I want to thank you _____.

3 Start a thank-you chain. One student thanks someone in the class. Then that student thanks someone else to continue the chain.

John, I want to thank you for sharing your notes with me.

4 Working on content

1 Look at Tony's notes about someone he would like to thank.

The person I want to thank	Kevin, my co-worker
What the person did	I was too embarrassed to tell the boss why I was late, so Kevin told her for me.
Why I am thankful	He understood that I felt bad. He helped me with my problem.

2 Choose someone who did something nice for you and who you would like to thank. Complete the chart.

The person I want to thank	
What the person did	
Why I am thankful	

3 Take turns asking a classmate these questions.

- Who is the person you want to thank?
- What nice thing did _____ do for you?
  (name)
- Why are you thankful?

4 Write about why you are thankful. Begin with *Thank you so much for . . . .*

Thank you so much for helping me at work. You understood how I felt, and you helped me with my problem.

5 Learning more about organization

TIME MARKERS
Use time markers such as *before*, *while*, and *after* in your writing to organize the events in your story.

1 Use the pictures to help you put the sentences below in order. Write the letters on the lines.

a While I was unlocking the front door, they hid behind the sofa and chairs.

b Before I got home, my friends brought a cake to my house and put up a sign.

c After I came in and turned on the light, all of my friends shouted, "Happy birthday!"

_____ _____ _____

2 Complete the story with *before*, *while*, or *after*.

There is an old man I want to thank for giving me his jacket. One evening ___after___ school, I walked to the bus stop. _____ I got to the bus stop, it started to rain, but I did not have an umbrella. _____ I was waiting for the bus, I got wetter and wetter. About 10 minutes _____ the bus came, an old man walked up to the bus stop. He saw how wet I was, so he took off his jacket and gave it to me _____ we were talking. Even today, _____ so many years, I am still grateful to that man for his kindness.

3 Look again at Part 4. Write three sentences about the nice thing someone did for you. Use *before*, *while*, and *after*.

a _____

b _____

c _____

6 Analyzing a model

1 You are going to write a thank-you note. First, read Tony's note and follow the instructions below.

> Hi Kevin,
>
> Thank you so much for helping me at work yesterday. After I got up, I went to work, but I was late. While I was working at my desk, I looked at the boss. She looked a little angry, but we didn't say anything to each other. I didn't tell her why I was late. Then, just before lunch, you told her that I worked on our sales report until four in the morning. You explained that I had trouble getting up because I was so tired, and that is why I was late. She didn't look angry after that. I wanted to tell her myself, but I was too embarrassed. So when you told her, it helped me a lot. Thank you so much for your kindness, Kevin. You understood that I felt bad, and you helped me with my problem.
>
> Your friend,
>
> Tony

a Underline the sentence that explains why Tony is writing the thank-you note.

b Put a star (✱) above each time marker.

c Check (✓) two other sentences that Tony could add to his note.

☐ Let me thank you by taking you out to lunch sometime.

☐ Next time, don't say anything.

☐ I love you.

☐ I'm lucky to have a friend like you.

2 Compare answers with a partner.

7 Write!

1 Plan your thank-you note.

    a Include a greeting (begin with *Hi* or *Dear*).

    _____

    b Write what you want to thank this person for.

    _____

    c Write sentences about what happened (use *before*, *while*, and *after*).

    _____

    _____

    _____

    _____

    d Include a closing for your note and your name.

    _____

    _____

2 Now write your thank-you note.

In your journal . . .

Write about a nice thing you did for someone. What was the situation? Why did you decide to do it? How did that person feel? How did you feel? Would you do it again?

8 Editing

Before, while, and *after* can be used in the middle or at the beginning of a sentence. Note the use of commas.

I wasn't happy before I met you.	↔	*Before I met you, I wasn't happy.*
You made dinner while I was working.	↔	*While I was working, you made dinner.*
I ate lunch after you lent me money.	↔	*After you lent me money, I ate lunch.*

1 Read each pair of sentences. Then rewrite the sentences using *before, while,* or *after.*

a I was happy. I talked to you on the phone.

<u>I was happy after I talked to you on the phone.</u>

b I felt better. I got your advice.

_____

c You lent me some money. I didn't know how generous you were.

_____

d You listened to me. I was practicing my speech.

_____

e I did not know how to solve my problem. I heard your advice.

_____

f You heard that I was in the hospital. You called me.

_____

g I was having trouble with my family. You called me every day and listened to my problems.

_____

2 Now look at the thank-you note you wrote in Part 7. See if you can improve your sentences.

9 Giving feedback

1 Exchange your revised thank-you note with a partner. Read your partner's revised thank-you note and follow the instructions below.

    a Did your partner include these things? Check (✓) the boxes.

	Yes	No
A greeting	☐	☐
The reason for writing	☐	☐
Some details about what happened	☐	☐
Sentences with time markers	☐	☐
A closing and a signature	☐	☐

    b Circle one or two sentences that are true. You can also write your own sentence.

        My partner seems kind and warmhearted.

        The person my partner wrote about seems kind and warmhearted.

        I want my partner to explain the note to me.

2 Write a short letter to your partner. Write something you like and a question you have. Then give the letter to your partner.

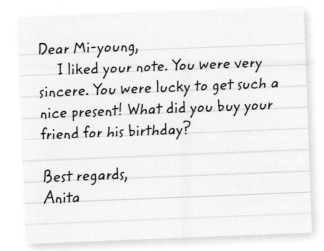

Dear Mi-young,
    I liked your note. You were very sincere. You were lucky to get such a nice present! What did you buy your friend for his birthday?

Best regards,
Anita

3 Can any of your partner's comments help you make your thank-you note better?

JUST FOR FUN

1 Write a thank-you card to someone at your school or in your neighborhood. Look at these examples.

a school staff member	a cleaning person	another teacher
a bus driver	a local shop owner	a nearby restaurant

2 Now fill in the chart.

	Example	Your idea
Name (or description) of the person	An older man in a blue work suit working in front of the school every morning. Maybe he is the school gardener?	
Why you want to thank that person	He always says good morning to me.	

3 Now write a thank-you card and give it to that person. Follow the example. Later, tell the class what happened.

> Hi,
>
> I want to thank you for being so friendly to me and the other students. Every morning, when I come to school, you smile and say, "Good Morning. How are you today?" That makes me smile. I usually don't feel very cheerful in the morning. After I see you, I always feel good. You make my hard day at school a little easier.
>
> After I graduate and go back to my home country, I will remember many good things about our school. You will be one of my good memories. So again, thank you.
>
> Your friend,
> Fahim Al Harbia

Movie review

1 Brainstorming

1 Do you know these movies? Match the pictures to the movie titles. Then check your answers at the bottom of the next page.

1	4
2	5
3	6

_____ **a** *Toy Story*

_____ **b** *The Lord of the Rings*

_____ **c** *Star Wars*

_____ **d** *The Dark Knight*

_____ **e** *Jurassic Park*

_____ **f** *Pirates of the Caribbean*

2 What movies have you seen recently? Brainstorm and make a list.

Movies

Slumdog Millionaire

3 Compare lists with a partner. Can you add more movies to your list?

> ### Later in this unit . . .
>
> You will write a movie review.
>
> You will also learn how to summarize a movie and include an opinion.

2 Analyzing a paragraph

1 Read the paragraph and follow the instructions below.

(1) <u>Avatar</u> is a movie about what happens to an alien planet when humans attack it. (2) The main characters of the movie are Jake, played by Sam Worthington, and Neytiri, played by Zoe Saldana. (3) Jake, an ex-soldier, falls in love with Neytiri, who lives on the beautiful planet Pandora. (4) The main message of <u>Avatar</u> is that we must try to understand other cultures.

a Put a star (✱) above the names of the characters and two stars (✱✱) above the names of the actors.

b Put a check (✓) above the phrase that explains what the movie is trying to say or teach the audience.

c Look at sentence 1 in the paragraph. Write a similar sentence with these words.

  Toy Story 3 / what happens to toys / their owner grows up

  _____

  _____

d Look at sentence 4 in the paragraph. Write a similar sentence with these words.

  main message / *Toy Story 3* / we can solve problems if we work together

  _____

  _____

2 Compare answers with a partner.

Talk about it.

Tell your partner about a movie that is similar to *Avatar*.

Answers to Step 1 on page 71
a3 b1 c6 e5 f4
d2

3 Learning about organization

MOVIE SUMMARY

The first part of a movie review is often a summary of the movie. The summary explains what the movie is about. It has three parts:

- the characters and actors
- the plot
- the message

1 Look at your brainstorming list from Part 1. Then choose a movie to review and write it here.

_____

2 Read the parts of three movie summaries and follow the instructions.

The characters and actors

Robin Hood, played by Russell Crowe, falls in love with Marion, played by Cate Blanchett.

a Write about the characters and actors in your movie.

_____

_____

The plot

Titanic is a movie about a ship that sinks. It is based on a true story. The Titanic hits some ice, and when it goes down, most of the passengers die.

b Write the plot of your movie.

_____

_____

The message

The message of Shutter Island is that the things we think are true are sometimes not true.

c Write the message of your movie.

_____

_____

4 Learning more about organization

MOVIE OPINION

You can give your opinion of the movie in the second part of your movie review. You can:

- discuss whether the movie and the acting are good or bad
- give a recommendation

1 Read the movie review and divide it into two paragraphs. Draw a line where the first paragraph ends, and the second paragraph begins.

Bend It Like Beckham tells the story of a women's soccer team in England. Parminder Nagra plays Jess, a girl whose parents don't think girls should play professional soccer. However, Jess is very good, and she continues playing. In the end, her parents recognize her talent and understand how much she wants to play. The message of the movie is that you should follow your dream. Bend It Like Beckham was very entertaining. There was action, drama, romance, and humor. I thought all of the actors were very good. The characters were believable, and I could understand the feelings of both Jess and her family. I learned a lot about soccer and English culture, too. I highly recommend this movie. Even if you are not interested in sports, you will love it!

2 Read more sentences from the movie review. In which paragraph do they belong? Write *1* for paragraph 1 and *2* for paragraph 2.

_____ **a** They want her to act more like other girls.

_____ **b** The soccer scenes were really exciting.

_____ **c** The music was also wonderful.

_____ **d** At first, her parents were angry with her.

3 Think about the movie you chose in Part 3. Circle the word or words that describe it. You can write your own words.

| entertaining | funny | slow | unbelievable | _____ |
| exciting | scary | touching | violent | _____ |

5 Working on content

1 Interview a partner.

   a Ask your partner about the movie he or she chose in Part 3. Ask
   questions like these.

   b Ask your partner's opinion of the movie he or she chose in Part 3. Ask
   questions like these.

   - What did you like or dislike about the movie?
   - Were the actors good?
   - Do you recommend this movie? Why or why not?

2 Now write your opinion of the movie you chose in Part 3. Follow
the example.

I think the movie Shrek is a really funny movie. Shrek and his wife,
Fiona, are an interesting couple. Shrek gets into trouble because he's simple
and strong, but Fiona always helps him. She is smart and understanding.
I liked both of the characters very much. I also really liked the voices the
actors gave the characters. I recommend that you see this movie.

_____

_____

_____

_____

_____

_____

6 Analyzing a model

1 You are going to write a movie review. First, read Jun's movie review and follow the instructions below.

> Slumdog Millionaire is a movie about a poor boy who gets rich on a TV show. It is based on a novel written by an Indian writer. The main characters are Jamal, played by Dev Patel, and Latika, played by Freida Pinto. Jamal was born in a slum in India. He has many troubles and adventures during his life, but finally he has a chance to get rich on a TV quiz show. However, he must also save Latika, his true love, from criminals. In the end, he wins a million dollars and saves her, and they escape together. The message of Slumdog Millionaire is that people from the slums have hard lives, but they can still do great things, especially when they trust their love.
>
> I think Slumdog Millionaire is a great movie. It is a happy story, but it teaches us a lot about poor people in India, and also about love. When I saw the movie, I really liked Jamal and Latika. I think everyone should see this wonderful movie.

a Underline the topic sentence in each paragraph.

b Mark these parts with numbers:

    1 actors' names   **3** opinion of the movie

    2 movie's message   **4** recommendation

c Put a star (✱) above the two past tense verbs in the second paragraph. Do you know why these verbs are in past tense?

d Which of these sentences is most similar to the movie's message? Check (✓) it.

    ☐ Anyone can fall in love if they try.
    ☐ Anyone can succeed if they try.
    ☐ Anyone can go on a quiz show if they try.

2 Compare answers with a partner.

7 Write!

1 Plan your movie review.

   a Write these things in the first paragraph.

Paragraph 1: The summary

A topic sentence: _____

The characters and actors: _____

_____

_____

The plot: _____

_____

_____

The message: _____

_____

_____

---

   b Write these things in the second paragraph.

Paragraph 2: My opinion

A topic sentence: _____

What you liked and did not like: _____

_____

_____

Whether you recommend the movie or not: _____

_____

_____

---

2 Now write your movie review.

In your journal . . .

Write about the kinds of movies you like best. Are there any kinds of movies that you don't like? Why?

8 Editing

1 Read the paragraph below. Change the underlined names to pronouns or possessive adjectives.

One message of the *Harry Potter* movies is that good friends are important. Harry has many problems in Harry's life. Harry is always in danger. However, Harry solves Harry's problems because Harry has some good friends to help Harry. The good friends are not typical kids. The good friends know magic and have some special skills. Harry's best friend is Ron. Ron is loyal and dependable. Ron often helps Harry get out of danger. Harry's other good friend is Hermione. Hermione is very smart and good at Hermione's studies. Hermione helps Harry with Harry's homework. Harry depends a lot on Ron and Hermione, and Ron and Hermione help Harry through many adventures. Harry, Ron, and Hermione's friendship is one of my favorite things about the movies.

2 Now look at the movie review you wrote in Part 7. See if you can improve your sentences.

9 Giving feedback

1 Work in groups of three or four. Exchange your revised movie review with members of another group.

a Read all of the other group's revised reviews and write a comment for each movie. Read the examples.

great acting   lots of action   good for children   scary

Name of movie	Your comment

b Now choose one movie review to give feedback on. Check (✓) the boxes.

	Yes	No
Does the review have two paragraphs?	☐	☐
Does the review explain the plot?	☐	☐
Does the review explain the characters?	☐	☐
Does the review explain the message?	☐	☐
Does the review include the writer's opinion about the movie?	☐	☐
Does the review include a recommendation to see or not see the movie?	☐	☐

c Write a short letter to your classmate. Write something you like and a question you have. Then give the letter to your classmate.

> Dear Sabrina,
>   I read your review of the movie Dark Knight, and I liked it very much. I especially liked the way you told the plot of the movie and how you described the Joker. Do you think . . . ?

2 Can any of your classmate's comments help you make your movie review better?

JUST FOR FUN

1 Produce a movie with your classmates. Form small groups of three or four. Give your movie a title. Write it here.

_____

2 Write your ideas for the movie's plot.

_____

_____

_____

_____

_____

3 Complete the chart. Write the names of the characters and the actors.

Characters	Actors

4 Make a movie poster. Follow the example.

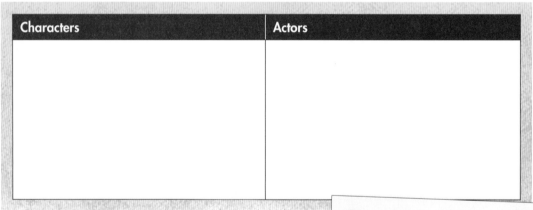

5 When you finish, hold a movie press conference.

   a One member of the group interviews the actors. Use the questions from Part 5.

   b Other members of the group play the actors answering questions about the new movie.

The New Snow White

Starring
Kate Hudson and **Susan Sarandon**

Kate Hudson plays Snow White and Susan Sarandon plays the evil stepmother. When the stepmother asks her magic mirror who the best karaoke singer in the world is, the mirror tells her it is Snow White. The stepmother decides to get rid of her.

Friendship

1 Brainstorming

1 What are the qualities of a good friend? Complete the sentences with words from the box.

> ☐ dependable   ☐ generous   ☑ kind
> ☐ funny   ☐ honest   ☐ loyal

a A friend who is caring and helpful is _____kind_____.

b A friend who makes you laugh is _____.

c A friend you can rely on is _____.

d A friend who tells you the truth is _____.

e A friend who is happy to spend time and money to

    help you is _____.

f A friend who always supports you is _____.

2 Who are your friends? What good qualities do they have? Brainstorm and make two lists. Use words from Step 1 above or your own ideas.

My friends	Their good qualities
Lisa	dependable, honest
Josh	cheerful, generous

3 Compare lists with a partner. Can you add more words to your lists?

> ### ▶ Later in this unit . . .
>
> You will write about a friend.
>
> You will also learn how to write supporting sentences.

2 Analyzing a paragraph

1 Read the paragraph and follow the instructions below.

(1) Lisa is a very good friend of mine. (2) She's dependable and honest. (3) She is there whenever I need someone to talk to, and she always tells me the truth. (4) She is also very funny. (5) If I am sad, Lisa makes me feel better with her jokes.

a Put a star (✱) above the three qualities that make Lisa a good friend.

b Underline three phrases that give examples of Lisa's qualities.

c Look at sentence 1 in the paragraph. Write a similar sentence with these words.

Josh / best friend

_____

_____

d Look at sentence 2 in the paragraph. Write a similar sentence with these words.

Josh / cheerful / generous / friendly

_____

_____

2 Compare answers with a partner.

Talk about it.

Tell your partner about a friend you share your problems with.

3 Working on content

1 What qualities do you think are very important, or not so important, in a friend? Check (✓) the boxes.

FRIENDSHIP CHART

		Very important	Not so important
a	Your friend is a good listener: He or she pays attention when you are talking.	☐	☐
b	Your friend is considerate: He or she remembers your birthday and special events in your life.	☐	☐
c	Your friend is secure in your friendship: He or she doesn't get jealous if you see other friends.	☐	☐
d	Your friend is sensitive: He or she always knows when you are upset.	☐	☐
e	Your friend is trustworthy: He or she doesn't tell your secrets to others.	☐	☐
f	Your friend is similar to you in clothing tastes: He or she dresses like you.	☐	☐
g	Your friend is forgiving: He or she knows that sometimes you make mistakes.	☐	☐
h	Your friend is fun: You can be silly and crazy as well as serious with your friend.	☐	☐
i	Your friend is punctual: He or she is always on time.	☐	☐

2 Look again at your brainstorming list from Part 1. Choose a friend you would like to write about. Write three good qualities that your friend has.

My friend's name   **Three good qualities**

Andrew_____   trustworthy_____ , respectful_____ , fun_____

_____   _____ , _____ , _____

4 Learning about organization

After you describe someone's good qualities, use supporting sentences to give examples.

Good quality: *Brandon is a good listener.*

Supporting sentence: *When I have a problem, he listens carefully.*

Supporting sentence: *He always lets me finish what I want to say before he speaks.*

1 Complete the sentences about good qualities with the names of people you know. Then write supporting sentences.

a _Andrew_____ is trustworthy.

Supporting sentence: _He never tells my secrets to others._____

b _____ is generous.

Supporting sentence: _____

c _____ is kind.

Supporting sentence: _____

d _____ is loyal.

Supporting sentence: _____

e _____ is fun.

Supporting sentence: _____

2 Now write about the good qualities of the friend you chose in Part 3. Then write supporting sentences.

a Good quality: _____

Supporting sentence: _____

b Good quality: _____

Supporting sentence: _____

c Good quality: _____

Supporting sentence: _____

5 Working more on content

1 Look at these examples of nice things people would like to do for their friends. Think of something special you would like to do for your friend. Then complete the sentence below.

I would like to _____.

2 Write notes about the nice thing you would like to do for your friend. Follow the example.

My friend	Naoki
I would like to . . .	take Naoki to a soccer game.
Explanation	Naoki loves soccer. He was a member of the soccer team when he was a high school student, and that is all he talks about. Once he even bought me a T-shirt at a soccer game. Next month, there will be an important soccer game in a city nearby. I would like to buy tickets for the game and take him because that would make him very happy!

My friend	
I would like to . . .	
Explanation	

3 Show your chart to a partner. Is there anything you want to add or change?

6 Analyzing a model

1 You are going to write about one of your friends. First, read Jane's paragraphs and follow the instructions below.

My Friend Carla

Carla, one of my best friends, is honest, dependable, and trustworthy. She is honest because she always tells me the truth about everything – even about how I look. She is dependable because she always does what she says she is going to do. Finally, Carla is trustworthy. She never tells anyone the secrets I tell her.

Carla is far away from her home in Brazil now, and the winter holidays are coming. I think it will be a lonely time for her, so I would like to invite her to come and stay at my house with my family. I think she will enjoy learning about our customs and teaching us about hers. I hope the two weeks we spend together will help us stay friends forever, even after she goes back to Brazil.

a Underline the topic sentence in the first paragraph.

b Circle the three good qualities Carla has.

c Put a star (✱) above the sentences that give examples of her good qualities.

d Draw a box around the topic sentence in the second paragraph that tells what Jane would like to do for Carla.

e Look at the title at the top of Jane's paragraph. Check (✓) two other titles that Jane could use.

☐ Carla, My Friend   ☐ Making a New Friend
☐ Taking a Friend to My Home   ☐ She is Trustworthy

2 Compare answers with a partner.

7 Write!

1 Plan your paragraphs about your friend. Remember to write these things in your paragraphs.

Paragraph 1: My friend

- a topic sentence about your friend's good qualities
- examples of these good qualities

Paragraph 2: Something I would like to do for my friend

- a topic sentence about what you would like to do for your friend
- the reasons why

2 Add a title to your paper.

a Make it simple. You don't need a period (.) at the end. Correct this title:

I Have a Friend Whose Name Is Charlie.

_____

b Capitalize the first letters in all the nouns, verbs, and content words, like *Friend*, *John*, *Home*, but not the articles and short prepositions. Correct this title:

Introducing Joan To A Friend In Vietnam

_____

c Capitalize the first letter of the title no matter what kind of word it is. Correct this title:

a New Friend I Made

_____

d Write your title at the top of your paper in the center.

3 Now write two paragraphs about your friend.

In your journal . . .

Write about the kind of friend you are. What are your best qualities?

8 Editing

To show a result, you can combine sentences with *so*. Use a comma after
the first sentence and before *so*.

Result

I think it will be a lonely time for Carla.   I would like to invite her to my house.

I think it will be a lonely time for Carla, so I would like to invite her to my house.

1 Read the pairs of sentences. Check (✓) the result. Then rewrite each pair as
one sentence with *so*.

a ☐ Naoki loves soccer.

☑ I want to take Naoki to a soccer game.

Naoki loves soccer, so I want to take
him to a soccer game.

b ☐ Cristina never tells secrets.

☐ I know I can trust Cristina.

c ☐ Eduardo knows a lot about me.

☐ I have known Eduardo since we were six.

d ☐ I am lonely.

☐ My best friend moved away.

e ☐ I will lend Ryan some money.

☐ Ryan needs to buy a new car.

f ☐ Sara loves computer games.

☐ I will buy Sara some new software.

2 Now look at the paragraphs you wrote in Part 7. See if you can improve your sentences.

9 Giving feedback

1 Exchange your revised paragraphs with a partner. Read your partner's revised paragraphs and follow the instructions below.

a Did your partner include these things? Check (✓) the boxes.

	Yes	No
a topic sentence for the first paragraph	☐	☐
a topic sentence for the second paragraph	☐	☐

b Complete the chart about your partner's friend. Use words or phrases, not sentences.

The friend's good qualities	Supporting words and phrases
honest	isn't afraid to disagree

c Circle one word to describe your partner's friend. You can write your own word.

fun   interesting   loyal   unusual   warm   _____

d What would your partner like to do for his or her friend? Write it here.

_____

_____

2 Write a short letter to your partner. Write something you like and a question you have. Then give the letter to your partner.

3 Can any of your partner's comments help you make your paragraphs better?

Dear Mayuko,
   I really liked reading about how you met your friend Hee-Young and what she is like. She sounds like a good friend and a good tennis player! How long have you known her?

Your friend,
Victor

1 Write an article about a classmate. First, read the article about Monica.

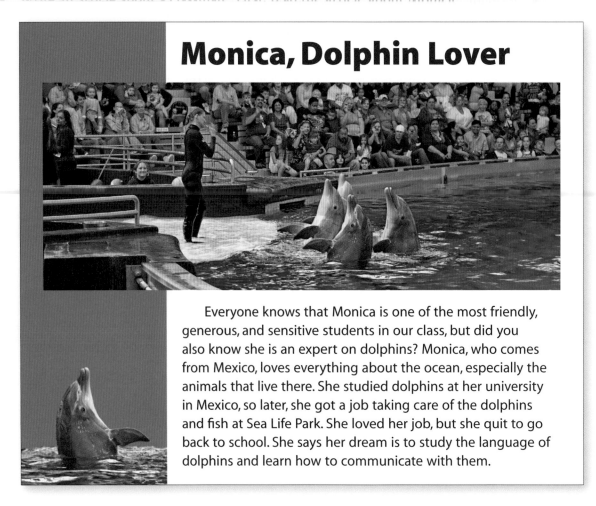

Monica, Dolphin Lover

Everyone knows that Monica is one of the most friendly, generous, and sensitive students in our class, but did you also know she is an expert on dolphins? Monica, who comes from Mexico, loves everything about the ocean, especially the animals that live there. She studied dolphins at her university in Mexico, so later, she got a job taking care of the dolphins and fish at Sea Life Park. She loved her job, but she quit to go back to school. She says her dream is to study the language of dolphins and learn how to communicate with them.

2 Interview a classmate. Find some interesting things to write about. Ask about topics like these.

dreams and future plans	family and friends	interests	job	life outside of school

3 Write three interesting things you've learned about your classmate.

_____, _____, _____

4 Write the article. Then show it to your classmate to make sure the information is correct. Make any necessary changes.

5 Write a title for your article.

_____

6 Draw a picture of your classmate or ask your classmate to give you a photo to put in the article.

Superhero powers

1 Brainstorming

1 Look at these superhero powers. Match the words in the box to the pictures.

☑ become invisible	☐ fly	☐ see through walls
☐ breathe underwater	☐ read minds	☐ travel through time

a _____ b _____ c _become invisible_

d _____ e _____ f _____

2 What superhero powers would you like to have? Brainstorm and make a list.

I wish I could . . .

lift a train
see the future

3 Compare lists with a partner. Can you add more superhero powers to your list?

> ### Later in this unit . . .
>
> You will write about superhero powers.
>
> You will also learn how to add examples to wishes.

2 Analyzing a paragraph

1 Read the paragraph and follow the instructions below.

(1) I am often late for work because of traffic jams. (2) I wish I could fly. (3) If I could fly, I would be able to get to work on time. (4) I would fly to my office on the twelfth floor without using the elevator. (5) Then I would go into my office through the window.

a Underline the sentence that explains a problem.

b Look at sentence 3 in the paragraph. What does it do? Check (✓) the correct answer.

☐ begins a story
☐ describes a place
☐ explains how to solve a problem

c Look at sentence 2 in the paragraph. Write a similar sentence with these words.

wish / see the future

_____

_____

d Look at sentence 3 in the paragraph. Write a similar sentence with these words.

see the future / get rich

_____

_____

2 Compare answers with a partner.

Talk about it.

Tell your partner if you would like to be able to fly. Explain why or why not.

3 Working on content

1 Choose two superhero powers from the list.

☐ become invisible   ☑ fly   ☐ see through walls
☐ breathe underwater   ☐ read minds   ☐ travel through time

2 Write sentences about the powers that you chose in Step 1 above. Follow the example.

a _I wish I could fly._ _____

b _____

c _____

3 What do you think each wish means? Match the superpowers to the meanings. (There are no wrong answers!)

If you wish you could . . .

_____ **a** become invisible,

_____ **b** breathe underwater,

_____ **c** fly,

_____ **d** read minds,

_____ **e** see through walls,

_____ **f** travel through time,

it might mean you . . .

1 are bored and want something new.

2 are curious about what other people are doing.

3 are shy and don't like to be watched.

4 like to be alone.

5 need to escape from the pressure in your life.

6 worry about what other people think about you.

4 Tell a partner about a superhero power you wished for in Part 1. Your partner will tell you what this wish might mean. Do you agree?

> If you wish you could become invisible, it might mean you are shy and don't like to be watched.

> That's true. I feel nervous speaking in front of groups of people.

4 Working more on content

1 Read Karen's wishes about superhero powers. Then match the superhero powers to the problems they can solve. You can use each superhero power twice.

1 I wish I could fly.

2 I wish I could talk to animals.

3 I wish I could travel back in time.

__2__ **a** I can't communicate with my cat.

_____ **b** I want to meet Shakespeare.

_____ **c** I don't like to take the train.

_____ **d** I don't have enough money to buy airplane tickets to go abroad.

_____ **e** I want to tell the birds to be quieter in the morning.

_____ **f** I hurt someone badly when I was a high school student.

2 What superhero powers would you like to have? What problems can they solve? Complete the chart.

I wish I could . . .	Why . . .
I wish I could talk to animals.	I can't communicate with my cat.

3 Interview your partner about his or her powers. Ask questions like these.

- What superhero powers did you choose?
- Why? What problems can they solve?

5 Learning about organization

Explain the superpower you wish you had. Then add examples of what you would do with it.

Wish: *I wish I could talk to animals.*

Examples of what you would do: *If I could talk to animals, I would communicate with Ginger, my cat. I would ask her why she sleeps all day.*

1 Read Karen's notes. Then write sentences from her notes. Use *could* and *would*.

      Things I would do if I could talk to animals:

- ask Ginger why she likes to chew on my shoes
- ask Ginger why she's afraid of the vacuum cleaner
- ask Ginger how she feels about mice
- teach Ginger how to use the TV

a If I could talk to animals, I would ask Ginger why she likes to chew on my shoes.

b _____

c _____

d _____

2 Choose a superhero power you wrote about in Part 4. Write notes about what you would do with this power.

      Things I'd do if I could _____:

- _____
- _____
- _____
- _____

3 Now write sentences from your notes. Use *could* and *would*.

a _____

b _____

c _____

d _____

6 Analyzing a model

1 You are going to write about your superhero power. First, read about Karen's superhero power and follow the instructions below.

Talking to Ginger

I love my cat, Ginger, but we cannot communicate very well. When Ginger is hungry, she meows. When Ginger runs away, I call her. We talk to each other, but we can only communicate simple things. I often wonder what she is really thinking when she looks out the window. I wonder if she really understands when I tell her about my problems. I want to communicate more with Ginger, so I wish I could talk to animals.

If I could talk to animals, I would ask Ginger many questions and teach her useful things. I would ask her why she is afraid of the vacuum cleaner and how she feels about mice. I would teach her how to use the TV so that she could watch it when I am at work. I would also tell her about my new boss, and I would ask for Ginger's advice on how to talk to him. If we could communicate, we would be able to share the important things in our lives.

a Underline the topic sentence in each paragraph.

b Put a star (✱) above each of the questions Karen would ask or things she would teach with the superpower.

c What does the concluding sentence in each paragraph do? Check (✓) the correct answer.

Paragraph 1
☐ It explains a problem.
☐ It explains a way to solve a problem.
☐ It shows why Karen loves Ginger.

Paragraph 2
☐ It finishes the story about Ginger.
☐ It adds more details.
☐ It explains why the superhero power is important to Karen.

2 Compare answers with a partner.

7 Write!

1 Plan your paragraphs about your superhero power.

a Write these things in your first paragraph.

Paragraph 1: My problem and the superhero power I would like
A topic sentence (explain your problem): _____
_____
_____
Additional details about your problem: _____
_____
_____
A concluding sentence (the superhero power you wish you had and why):
_____
_____

b Write these things in your second paragraph.

Paragraph 2: What I would do with the superhero power
A topic sentence (explain what you would do with the power):
_____
_____
A concluding sentence (explain why the power is important to you):
_____
_____

2 Put a title, like the one on page 96, at the top.

3 Now write your paragraphs about your superhero power.

In your journal . . .

Write about a superhero who you liked when you were a child. Describe the superhero's powers and what the superhero did with them. Tell what you would do if you could be like that person.

8 Editing

1 Read the wishes on the Wish Tree. Complete the sentences with *want, were, could,* or *would*.

Wish Tree

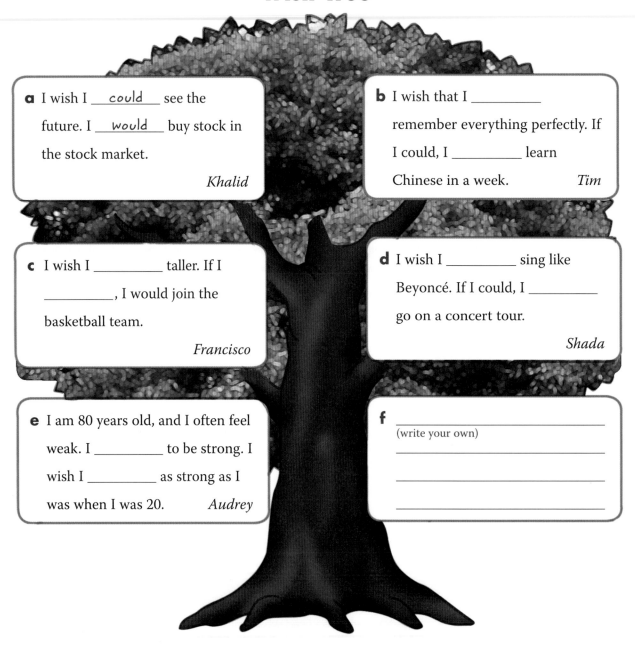

a I wish I __could__ see the future. I __would__ buy stock in the stock market.

Khalid

b I wish that I _____ remember everything perfectly. If I could, I _____ learn Chinese in a week.   *Tim*

c I wish I _____ taller. If I _____, I would join the basketball team.

Francisco

d I wish I _____ sing like Beyoncé. If I could, I _____ go on a concert tour.

Shada

e I am 80 years old, and I often feel weak. I _____ to be strong. I wish I _____ as strong as I was when I was 20.   *Audrey*

f _____

(write your own)

_____

_____

_____

2 Now look at the paragraphs you wrote in Part 7. See if you can improve your sentences.

9 Giving feedback

1 Imagine that you are a member of an awards committee. You are awarding prizes for the most interesting superhero powers. Follow the instructions below.

a Work in groups of four. Exchange your revised paragraphs with a classmate in another group. Read your classmate's revised paragraphs and complete the chart.

Superhero power	What problems it could solve	What the person would do

b Tell your group about the superhero power you read about. Discuss each superhero power and vote for the best one. Write it here.

Best superhero power: _____

c Give awards to the other superhero powers. Choose from the awards below or write your own idea.

Most unusual: _____

The funniest: _____

Most practical: _____

_____
(your idea)

2 Write a short letter to your classmate. Write something you like and a question you have. Then give the letter to your classmate.

3 Can any of your classmate's comments help you make your paragraphs better?

Dear Karen,
   I like your idea. If you want to talk to animals, it might mean that communication is very important to you. Do you think your cat wants to talk to you, too?

Your classmate,
Allie

JUST FOR FUN

1 Make up a group of superheroes and write a comic book story about them. Follow the instructions.

    a Work with a partner and create a superhero or a group of superheroes.

    b Give each superhero a special power.

    c Create a criminal character, too. Give the criminal character a superhero power.

Time Man can time travel.

XYZ can see the future.

Dr. Cruel can control people's feelings.

2 Think of a story for your characters. Write notes. Follow the example.

Part 1   Introduce Time Man and XYZ.
Part 2   Dr. Cruel makes farmers want to give him their land. They do.
Part 3   XYZ sees the future. Dr. Cruel is rich. The farmers are poor and homeless.
Part 4   Time Man goes back into the past to tell the farmers not to give away their land.

3 Choose one of the parts above to draw. Include dialogs and narration.

Dr. Cruel is trying to take land from the farmers.

XYZ and Time Man decide to help the farmers.

Advertisements

1 Brainstorming

1 What advertising claims do these products make? Match the products to
the claims.

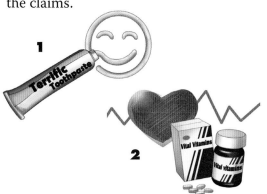

Super Sonic Sneaker

TATER chips

Advertising claims

_____ **a** Run faster and jump higher!   _____ **b** Have a beautiful smile!

_____ **c** Stop your hunger!   _____ **d** Feel stronger and look younger!

2 What are products and claims you've seen in advertisements? Brainstorm
and make two lists.

Products	Advertising claims
Palma Shampoo	have softer hair

3 Compare lists with a partner. Can you add more to your lists?

> ### Later in this unit . . .
>
> You will write an advertisement.
>
> You will also learn how to include attention getters
> and testimonials.

2 Analyzing a paragraph

1 Read the paragraph and follow the instructions below.

Barefoot Joggers

(1) Imagine running shoes that are so comfortable you'll want to sleep in them. (2) Barefoot Joggers are the lightest and most comfortable shoes ever made. (3) If you wear these running shoes, you'll run faster and jump higher. (4) Your friends will be amazed. (5) Take off your old, uncomfortable shoes and try Barefoot Joggers today!

a Put a star (✱) above each quality of the Barefoot Joggers.

b Put a check (✓) above the phrases that tell the good things that will happen to you if you buy the product.

c Look at sentence 2 in the paragraph. Write a similar sentence with these words.

Lightning Coffee / powerful

_____

_____

d Look at sentence 5 in the paragraph. Write a similar sentence with these words.

weak / old coffee / Lightning Coffee

_____

_____

2 Compare answers with a partner.

Talk about it.

Tell your partner about your favorite products, such as your favorite kinds of shampoo, shoes, clothes, or cars.

3 Working on content

1 When you write an advertisement, you will want to include a claim and a recommendation. Complete the recommendations with words from the Word File.

    a _____Wear_____ these running shoes.

    b _____ just one potato chip.

    c _____ this toothpaste after meals.

    d _____ one vitamin every morning at breakfast.

<table>
<tr><td>Word File</td></tr>
<tr><td>☐ to taste</td></tr>
<tr><td>☐ to take</td></tr>
<tr><td>☐ to use</td></tr>
<tr><td>☑ to wear</td></tr>
</table>

2 Match the recommendations in Step 1 above to the results in the box to make advertising claims about the products. Rewrite the claims below.

☐ You will have a beautiful smile.	☐ You will feel stronger and look younger.
☑ You will run faster and jump higher.	☐ You will want to eat them all.

    a _If you wear these running shoes, you will run faster and jump higher._

    b _____

    c _____

    d _____

3 Think of a product you would like to make, even one that is not possible yet. Complete the chart. Then write two advertising claims and a recommendation for your product.

What the product does	The name of the product
A special tool that measures how someone feels about you.	_The Love Meter_

Advertising claims: **a** _____

                           b _____

Recommendation: _____

4 Learning about organization

ATTENTION GETTERS

Attention getters make the reader want to read more. Advertisers use attention getters at the start of an advertisement to get the reader interested.

Attention getters:
- can be a sentence, a question, or just one word.
- are usually surprising or funny.
- can make you think about a problem you have.
- often appear with a picture.

1 Match the pictures to the attention getters.

_____ **a** If you like washing clothes, don't read this!

_____ **b** No more bad hair days!

_____ **c** True love, or just friends?

_____ **d** Paradise is wet.

2 Now write an attention getter for your product from Part 3. Then draw a picture of your product in the box.

Attention getter:

_____

_____

5 Learning more about organization

TESTIMONIALS

After your attention getter, it is often a good idea to include a testimonial.
A testimonial is a statement by someone who uses a product. Advertisers
often use testimonials to help sell their products.

"My teeth have never been brighter!"

"Now I get all of the vitamins I need."

1 Read the notes for the testimonial about the Perfect Sleep Pillow below.

Before using the Perfect Sleep Pillow	After using the Perfect Sleep Pillow
- had trouble getting to sleep - had boring dreams - looked terrible and was tired all the time	- now sleep perfectly and peacefully - have wonderful dreams - look and feel great all day

"I used to have trouble getting to sleep at night. I had boring dreams
and woke up many times during the night. I looked terrible in the
morning, and I was tired all the time. Then I tried the Perfect Sleep
Pillow. Now I sleep perfectly and peacefully, and I have wonderful
dreams, too. Best of all, I look and feel great in the morning!"

2 Complete the chart with notes for a testimonial about your product.

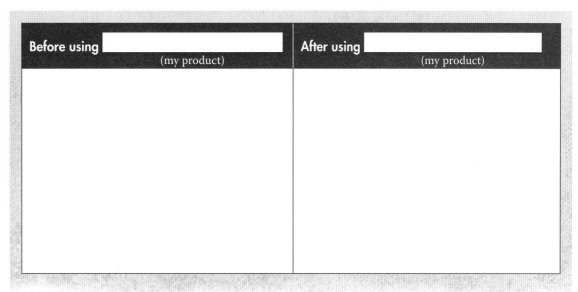

Before using _____ (my product)	After using _____ (my product)

3 Imagine you are a customer giving a testimonial about your product. Tell a
partner what it was like before and after using the product.

6 Analyzing a model

1 You are going to write an advertisement. First, read this advertisement and follow the instructions below.

True Love? Or Just Friends?

Do you ever wonder how that special person in your life *really* feels about you? Now you can find out.

"*I used to spend hours wondering if Josefina truly loved me. In fact, I couldn't concentrate on anything else. But now, thanks to the Love Meter, the answer is right in front of my face! Now I know the truth, and I feel a lot better.*"

True love was hard to find before, but not anymore! The Love Meter is the quickest, easiest, and most accurate way to measure love. If you point it at a co-worker, friend, or romantic partner and push the "love test" button, in three seconds you will learn whether that person loves you or not. The Love Meter is so small that it can be hidden in a pocket or bag, so your love interest won't see it. Buy the Love Meter and take it with you the next time you meet that special person.

a Look at the advertisement. Circle the attention getters in the first and second paragraphs.

b Look at the second paragraph.
- Underline the topic sentence.
- Put a star (✳) above the advertising claim.
- Draw a box around the sentence with the recommendation.

2 Compare answers with a partner.

7 Write!

1 Plan your advertisement.

a Write these things in the first paragraph.

First paragraph
An attention getter: _____
_____
A testimonial that explains what it was like before and after using the product:
_____
_____
_____
_____

b Write these things in the second paragraph.

Second paragraph
A topic sentence (with the name of the product and what kind of product it is):
_____
_____
What it can do (the advertising claims): _____
_____
A recommendation: _____
_____
_____
_____

2 Now write your advertisement. Include a drawing or photo of the customer or product.

In your journal . . .

Write about a product you bought because of an advertisement. What was it? Were you happy with it? Do you think the advertisement told the truth?

8 Editing

Advertisements try to persuade customers that a company's product is the best.

The superlative form of the adjective is often used.

the fastest car	*the silliest movie*
the hottest coffee	*the most beautiful watch*
the newest model	*the most exciting TV show*
the funniest book	*the most intelligent pet*

1 Complete the sentences with the superlative form of the adjectives in the box.

☐ big	☐ loud	☑ scary
☐ funny	☐ intelligent	☐ light

a Don't expect to sleep after reading this book because it has some of the
_____scariest_____ ghost stories ever written.

b The Giant Burger Deluxe is the _____ hamburger in
Australia! Just one is enough for your whole family.

c Get ready to laugh because once again, Lester Jester stars in the
_____ movie of the year.

d The Awake Alarm Clock is the _____ alarm clock in the
world. You won't be able to oversleep!

e A Leafbook Computer is the _____ computer you can
buy. It weighs less than two pounds.

f Some of the _____ people in the world read the
Newscast Web site.

2 Now look at the advertisement you wrote in Part 7. See if you can improve your sentences.

9 Giving feedback

1 Work in groups of three. Exchange your revised advertisement with members of another group. Read all of the other group's revised advertisements and follow the instructions.

a Complete the chart below about each product. Use words from the box or write your own words.

creative	fashionable	powerful	unusual	_____
cute	funny	relaxing	useful	_____

Product name	Three words to describe the product
Product 1 _____	_____, _____, _____
Product 2 _____	_____, _____, _____
Product 3 _____	_____, _____, _____

b Tell the members of the other group the words you chose for their products.

2 Choose one advertisement to give feedback on.

a Does the advertisement include these things? Check (✓) the boxes.

	Yes	No
an attention getter	☐	☐
the name of the product and what it is	☐	☐
a testimonial	☐	☐
some advertising claims about the product	☐	☐
a recommendation	☐	☐

b Write a short letter to the classmate whose advertisement you chose. Write something you like and a question you have. Then give the letter to your classmate.

> Dear Meg,
>   I liked your advertisement. I thought the testimonial was believable. I would like to buy some Lightning Coffee! How much does it cost?
>
> Your sleepy classmate,
> Tyler

3 Can any of your classmate's comments help you make your advertisement better?

JUST FOR FUN

1 Have a class market. Select three things that you have with you to pretend to sell. Write them on the lines below.

_____   _____   _____

2 Write brief advertisements for each item on separate pieces of paper. You might include:

- an attention getter
- an advertising claim
- a testimonial
- a recommendation

3 Display your items. Then look at your classmates' items and ask questions. Follow the example.

> I like those sunglasses. Are they in fashion this year?

> Oh, they're the most fashionable sunglasses around! If you wear them, people will think you are a movie star!

Lessons learned

1 Brainstorming

1 Look at actions people sometimes do that they regret or feel sorry about.
Check (✓) the ones that you dislike the most.

☐ telling secrets ☐ not listening ☐ losing something

☐ getting angry ☐ being late ☐ lying

2 What actions do you regret? Who did they hurt? Brainstorm and make two lists.

Actions	Who the actions hurt
I got angry	my sister

3 Compare lists with a partner. Can you add more things to your lists?

> **Later in this unit . . .**
>
> You will write about an action you regret.
>
> You will also learn how to write an explanation and a concluding paragraph.

2 Analyzing a paragraph

1 Read the paragraph and follow the instructions below.

(1) I regret that I lied to my father.
(2) Last month, I forgot that I was supposed to meet my father at the train station at 4:00.
(3) When I finally got there at 4:45, I told my father that my bus was late. (4) He knew it was not true, and he got angry. (5) I felt guilty, so I apologized and told him the truth.

a Sentence 1 is the topic sentence of the paragraph above. Check (✓) another sentence that could be the topic sentence of the paragraph.

☐ I have problems with being on time.
☐ I learned that I should tell the truth.
☐ I really liked talking to my father.

b Put a star (✱) above two words in the paragraph that describe people's feelings.

c Look at sentence 1 in the paragraph. Write a similar sentence with these words.

feel bad / told someone / friend's secret

_____

_____

d Look at sentence 5 in the paragraph. Write a similar sentence with these words.

ashamed / said I was sorry / promised to never tell her secrets again

_____

_____

2 Compare answers with a partner.

Talk about it.

Tell your partner what kinds of things you think it's okay to lie about.

3 Learning about organization

To explain an action you regret, write about the situation, what you did wrong, and the consequences of your actions.

The situation:	*I told my friend I would go to a movie with her.*
What I did wrong:	*I forgot and went to dinner with my family.*
The consequences:	*She was hurt. I promised to take her to a movie next week and pay for both of us.*

1 Complete the stories below with sentences from the box.

> ☐ My brother brought his friends into my room and used my computer.
> ☐ She was sad. I said I was sorry, and I'm going to take her to the movies tonight.
> ☐ I promised to never lie to her again. She forgave me, but I have to work late every Friday!
> ☐ I didn't have enough money, so I couldn't pay him back.

a **The situation:** Yesterday was my wife's birthday. She expected me to give her a present.

What I did wrong: I forgot to get her a present.

The consequences: _____

b **The situation:** I borrowed $100 from my friend last week. I promised to pay him back by today.

What I did wrong: _____

The consequences: I apologized, but he was still mad. When I told him I'd pay him $125 next week, he forgave me.

c **The situation:** _____

What I did wrong: I got angry and yelled at him.

The consequences: I apologized for getting angry, and he promised not to do it again. Now we're friends again.

d **The situation:** I told my boss I had to go home early because my husband was sick.

What I did wrong: I went out to lunch with my friends instead, and she found out.

The consequences: _____

2 Compare answers with a partner.

4 Working on content

1 Look again at your brainstorming list in Part 1. Choose an action you regret or feel sorry about. Write the action and who was hurt below.

_____   _____
(the action)   (who was hurt)

2 Look at Jenny's notes about her regret. Then complete the chart below about your regret.

The situation	Last winter, I borrowed my friend Ashley's scarf. It was her favorite scarf.
What I did wrong	I left it on the train.
The consequences	I felt guilty. I couldn't sleep. Ashley was sad, but she forgave me.

The situation	
What I did wrong	
The consequences	

3 Work in groups of three. Tell each other about your regret. Can you add more information to your chart?

5 Learning more about organization

CONCLUSIONS

After explaining something you regret, you might also write what you learned from it. This can be just a concluding sentence or a whole paragraph.

Be sure to consider the situation, what you did wrong, and the consequences. Then think about the lesson you learned.

1 Read this explanation. What lesson do you think this person learned? Check (✓) the best sentence.

I borrowed my roommate's car without asking. He got angry.

Lesson learned:
☐ I should ask permission before I borrow things.
☐ I shouldn't borrow things from my roommate.
☐ My roommate is mean.

2 Now read these explanations. Write a lesson learned.

a It usually takes me 20 minutes to get from my home to my job. Yesterday, I left home exactly 20 minutes before my job started. There was more traffic than usual, so I was 15 minutes late.

Lesson learned: _____

b Another student asked if he could copy my homework. I lent him my homework, and the teacher found out. She gave us both a zero on the homework.

Lesson learned: _____

c I promised to wash dishes and clean up the kitchen while my family went shopping. I watched TV instead. When they came home, they were upset.

Lesson learned: _____

d When I finished my job, $100 was missing. I lost it, so it was my fault. I sent my boss an e-mail saying that I was sorry, but he got angry. He said an apology was not enough, so I gave him $100.

Lesson learned: _____

3 Think about the action you regret from Part 4. Write one or more lessons you learned from it.

_____

_____

6 Analyzing a model

1 You are going to write about something you did that you regret and what you learned. First, read about Jenny's regret and follow the instructions below.

Something I Feel Bad About

I feel bad that I lost my friend Ashley's scarf. Ashley had a very beautiful and expensive scarf that she loved. She let me borrow it one day, and I promised to be careful with it. I wore it all day. It was very nice. Then I took it off while I was going home on the train. I left it on the train by mistake. I noticed that it was missing when I got home, so I called the station, but it was gone. I felt very guilty. I told Ashley that I was very sorry. I know that she was sad, but she smiled and said she wasn't angry.

That experience taught me two things. First, I learned that I must be more careful with other people's things. Second, Ashley taught me what true friendship is. She decided that our friendship was more important than getting angry at me. I am lucky to have a friend like her.

---

a Underline the topic sentence in each paragraph.

b Order the events. Write numbers (1–5) next to the events

<u> 1 </u> I borrowed a scarf.

_____ I apologized.

_____ Ashley didn't get angry.

_____ I left it on the train.

_____ I learned a lesson.

c Put a star (✱) above five words in the first paragraph that describe feelings.

d Circle the lessons that Jenny learned.

2 Compare answers with a partner.

7 Write!

1 Plan your paragraphs about something you regret and what you learned.

   a First, make a list of all the events. Use your notes from Part 4 and Part 5, but add more details.

   Example:

- Ashley's scarf was beautiful
- I asked her to lend it to me; she said "yes"
- I wore it all day
- I went home on the train
- I took it off
- I forgot it on the train
- I noticed when I got home
- I called the station, but they did not have it
- I told Ashley

   b Write these things:

- a paragraph about your regret (the situation, what you did wrong, the consequences)
- a paragraph about the lesson learned
- a topic sentence for each paragraph

2 Now write about your regret and what you learned.

In your journal . . .

Write about a time when someone did something bad to you. Write how you think that person felt.

8 Editing

1 Read the words in the box that describe good and bad feelings. Then write
the words in the correct list.

☑ angry ☐ depressed ☐ embarrassed ☑ proud
☐ ashamed ☐ disappointed ☐ excited ☐ relieved

Good feelings	Bad feelings
proud	angry

2 Complete the sentences with a word from the box in Step 1 above.

a I became so (*good feeling*) _____excited_____ that I dropped my friend's cell

phone. It broke. She was (*bad feeling*) _____angry_____. Why was I so careless?

b I'm so (*good feeling*) _____ that my friend forgave me. I thought
he might stay angry.

c After Gina said she never wanted to see me again, I was (*bad feeling*)
_____ for a long time. I didn't even want to leave my house.

d I thought my friend was an honest person, but I was (*bad feeling*)
_____ when she stole my MP3 player. She really let me down. I
cannot trust her anymore.

e When I forgot part of my speech in class, I was so (*bad feeling*) _____
that I could feel my face turn red. Why didn't I practice more?

f After I cheated on the test, I felt so (*bad feeling*) _____ that I told
the teacher. I felt (*good feeling*) _____ after that for being honest.

3 Now look at the paragraphs you wrote in Part 7. See if you can improve your sentences.

9 Giving feedback

1 Exchange your revised paragraphs with a partner. Read your partner's revised paragraphs and follow the instructions below.

a Write the action that your partner regrets or feels bad about.

_____

b How bad do you think the action was? Check (✓) your answer.

not very bad □────────□────────□ *very bad*

c How upset do you think the other person was? Check (✓) your answer.

not very upset □────────□────────□ *very upset*

d Did your partner include these things? Check (✓) the boxes.

	Yes	No
a topic sentence for each paragraph	□	□
who your partner upset	□	□
when the action happened	□	□
what your partner learned	□	□

2 Write a short letter to your partner. Write something you like and a question you have. Then give the letter to your partner.

Dear Eric,
    You did something bad to your neighbor's car, but I think you learned an important lesson. Are you friends with your neighbor again?

Best regards,
Takuma

3 Can any of your partner's comments help you make your paragraphs better?

JUST FOR FUN

1 Make a card with a poem about an action you regret or feel sorry about.
Follow the instructions.

a Complete the chart.

Who I will send the card to	What I regret

b Look at the example. Then write a funny or serious poem about your
action. Write the words at the ends of the second and fourth lines so they
rhyme like these words.

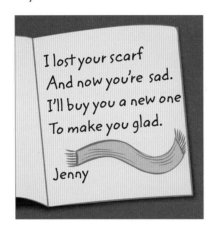

I lost your scarf
And now you're sad.
I'll buy you a new one
To make you glad.

Jenny

sad – glad   wrong – long
forget – regret   blame – shame

_____

_____
                              (rhyming word)

_____

_____
                              (rhyming word)

2 Now make the card. Fold a piece of paper twice like the example.

a Write the poem upside down in the top left
box. Sign your name, too.

b For the cover page, draw a picture and
write a phrase like one of these in the
lower right box.

- Oops!   ■ Forgive me!
- Sorry!   ■ Silly me!
- A big mistake! ■ I'm bad!

3 When you finish, display your cards on your
desks. Later, send your card to the person you
made it for.